# LAND OF FRANKINCENSE
## THE GUIDE TO THE HISTORY, LOCATIONS AND UNESCO SITES OF FRANKINCENSE IN DHOFAR OMAN

TONY WALSH

# CONTENTS

| | |
|---|---|
| Introduction | ix |
| 1. EXPLORERS OF DHOFAR | 1 |
| 2. BIOLOGY & MEDICINAL USE | 7 |
| Medicine | 14 |
| 3. HISTORY | 19 |
| 4. WADI DAWKAH UNESCO SITE | 35 |
| 5. HANUN | 43 |
| 6. ASH SHISR UNESCO SITE | 49 |
| 7. ANDHUR | 61 |
| 8. MUGHSAYL | 69 |
| 9. AYN HAMRAN FORT | 77 |
| 10. QASBAR FORT | 83 |
| 11. KHAWR RAWRI & SAMHARAM UNESCO SITE | 91 |
| Khawr Rawri and Samharam's physical sites | 104 |
| 12. AL BALID UNESCO SITE | 129 |
| Al Balid's physical sites | 144 |
| More Reading | 163 |
| Arabic Language | 165 |

# INTRODUCTION

Dhofar is a magically unexpected corner of Arabia. For almost 30 years, I travelled through this region, often with tourists travelling with my tour company. At other times I explored, alone or with friends, the mountains escarpments, places behind military checkpoints and into Yemen. Some of these off-the-beaten-track places in Dhofar were in the 5th Edition of the Oman guide I wrote for Bradt Guides; after all even though you might not use the international border into Yemen, it can scarcely be ignored in a nationwide guide book.

However, a guidebook format, such as the Oman guide, covering an entire country provides just a snippet of information about each location, and Dhofar deserves more. This guide to The Land of Frankincense offers my overview of the background of Frankincense, its Biology, natural Environment and History. Nine locations directly associated with Frankincense in Oman, including the four UNESCO World Heritage Sites are included in this book.

There are locations written about that can be reached by Tarmac road, others are Off-road, often on challenging tracks, or even no track at all. Take suitable precautions for your safety and those accompanying you, most especially understanding your vehicle's capability and your own as its driver. GPS locations in this book are a rough indication and not to be definitive or used for navigation. As with all such locational suggestions, accuracy can depend on your GPS device and that of all the transmitting satellites.

The purpose of providing text about medicinal treatment here is to present its historical context or illustrate how some people or organizations use or research Frankincense today. There is no intention of making any therapeutic suggestion, indeed I am not a medical doctor. Many of the substances are toxic. Do not medicate yourself; see a medical doctor.

I hope you enjoy exploring Dhofar with this book and the Bradt Guide to Oman; both are written in British English.

It will help other people get an insight about the book if you leave a review on the website of the retailer you purchased it from.

thank you 🙏
Tony.

# INTRODUCTION

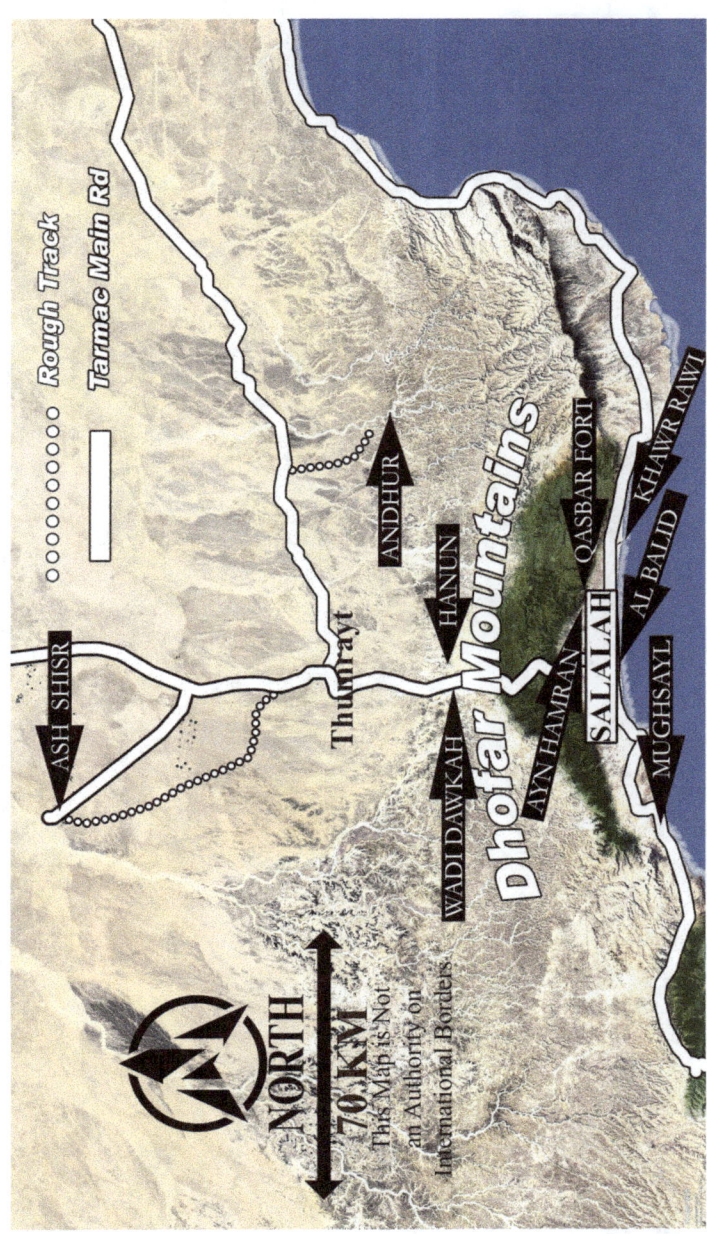

# CHAPTER 1
# EXPLORERS OF DHOFAR

**E**XPLORERS OF DHOFAR - BY TIME PERIOD
    **Marco Polo** lived from AD1254 –1324. He was born in Italy and set off on his travels in AD1271. His book 'The Travels of Marco Polo' purported to write about these travels. He wrote about Al Balid; however, whether he visited the town is doubtful. Though having visited Hormuz twice, he may have had good second-hand information about Al Balid from merchants at Hormuz.
    **Ibn Battuta** (also Ibn Battutah, Mohammed bin Abdullah Al Lawati) lived from AD 1304 – 1369. He was born in Tangier, Morocco and studied Islamic law. In 1325, he set off on the Islamic pilgrimage to Makkah, the 'Haj'. Instead of returning home, he continued travelling, often working as a judge, and marrying women from the cities where he stayed. He visited Al Balid in 1330, reached China in 1345, only returning home via Al Balid in 1347 and finally landing in Tangier in 1354. After returning home from his travels in 1354 he dictated an account of his journeys, mainly from his memory, to Mohammad Al Gharnati.
    **Zheng He** lived AD 1371-1435 and was an official for the early Ming Emperors of China. He made seven voyages as an Ambassador to the Oceans west of China with immense fleets of ships. They appear to have visited Al Balid on three voyages in

1418, 1422, and 1433. The fleets often segmented and made detours or advanced ahead of Zheng He's own flagship flotilla. Many of the records that his clerks had recorded were deliberately destroyed, by subsequent officialdom.

**Henry John Carter** lived from AD 1813 to 1895. He was born in Britain, but spent most of his working life in Bombay as a military surgeon. However, he gained renown for his work in geology and zoology, especially when working on the survey ship 'Palinurus' between AD1847-1857.

**Theodore & Mabel Bent** – Theodore lived AD 1852-1897 and was born in Britain, and Mabel, to whom he was married, was born in Wexford in what is now modern Ireland and lived AD1847-1929. They travelled together in the Near East, producing extensive reports and providing innumerable natural specimens collected in the areas they travelled through. In 1895, they arrived by sea from Karachi via Muscat into Dhofar, where they spent a few days exploring before leaving because of general unrest within the area.

*Bertram Thomas and his Guide Team - with Sheikh Salih bin Khalut on the right of Thomas (to his left as viewed here).*

**Bertram Thomas** lived from AD 1892 to 1950. He was born in Britain and served in the military during World War 1. In 1916, they transferred him to Iraq, then ruled by Britain. After the war, he became an Assistant Political Officer there during the establishment of the Kingdom of Iraq in 1921. In 1922, shortly after Jordan became a Kingdom, he received an appointment as Assistant British Representative (Assistant Ambassador) to Jordan. His involvement in Oman began when he was appointed effective Prime Minister and Finance Minister to Sultan Taimur Al Said in 1925. Bertram Thomas held this role until 1932, and his resignation. He wrote two books about Oman. 'Alarms and Excursions in Arabia', including travel in Musandam, the Batinah, and Dhofar. The second Book, Arabia Felix, focuses on his trailblazing journey from Dhofar through the Rub Al Khali to Doha in Qatar, the first time a non-Arab had achieved this. Most of his journeys in Oman were by Camel, and he was the only British person in them, relying entirely on his guides.

**Wilfred Thesiger** lived AD 1910–2003. He was born in Addis Ababa, Ethiopia, where his father was the British Ambassador. Educated at Eton College and Oxford University in Britain, he worked for the Sudan Government as an administrator for one of its vast provinces. He joined the British Army and the SAS (a special forces unit) in the Second World War.

Though from a privileged British background, Wilfred Thesiger gravitated towards less materially developed cultures, exploring areas in the Horn of Africa. Thesiger got a job researching the Desert Locusts in Southern Arabia in 1945. In the late 1940s, he travelled extensively through desert areas in Oman, Yemen, Saudi Arabia, and the UAE, guided by men from tribes in southern Oman. He wrote about his explorations in Arabian Sands and his later visits to Iraq in the Marsh Arabs.

**Wendell Phillips** lived AD 1921-1975 and was born in the USA. Getting a Bachelors degree in palaeontology, he served in the Merchant Marine in World War II. From 1949, Phillips excavated in Yemen before leaving for fear of attack in 1952. He undertook excavations in Dhofar from 1952-1962 with Dr William Albright 1891 1971, a biblical scholar. They removed the items excavated, and unfortunately, little accessible documentation of the results is available.

*Wilfred Thesiger and a Modern Omani Man*

**JURIS ZARINS** WAS BORN IN GERMANY. THE University of Chicago awarded Juris Zarins a PhD in archaeology, and he later became an advisor to the Department of Antiquities of the Kingdom of Saudi Arabia. Since 1990, he has surveyed several sites in Oman, including Ash Shisr.

**Nicholas Clapp** was born in the Los Angeles, USA. He had filmed the reintroduction of Oryx to Oman, and this experience was the magnet that created his desire to return to Oman. He conceived the idea of searching for the lost city of Ubar in 1981. He wrote a book about his search, from 1990, for Ubar, 'The Road to Ubar'.

**Ranulph Fiennes** was born in Britain. From 1963 to 1971, he was a soldier, spending the last two years in the Oman army. A lifetime of adventure includes a quieter search for Ubar from 1990, with Nicholas Clapp, which he wrote about as part of his 'Atlantis of the Sands'.

**University of Aachen - Michael Jansen**. The University of Aachen in Germany excavated Al Balid in 1994 under Dr Michael Jansen. Specialising in the Indus Valley, he had also conducted other work, including Afghanistan.

**University of Pisa - Alessandra Avanzini**. The University of Pisa and the Sultanate of Oman have been fortunate to have had excavations in Oman under the direction of Dr Alessandra Avanzini since 1996. She specialises in Southern Arabia and has created a substantial pool of experts in the Southern Arabia region at Pisa. Several specialized publications have resulted from her team's work in the northern Oman site of Salut and most extensively at Khawr Rawri, including 'A port in Arabia between Rome and the Indian Ocean'.

## CHAPTER 2
# BIOLOGY & MEDICINAL USE

**B**IOLOGY & MEDICINAL USE
Traders transported Frankincense resin throughout the ancient world, from Rome to China. It became an essential element in culture, religion, trade, and the growth of towns. On December 2nd, AD 2,000, the UNESCO World Heritage List added four sites in Oman associated with Frankincense. This book includes these sites, along with others.

~

THE ENGLISH NAME ORIGINATES FROM MIDDLE English, using the Old French *franc encens*: pure or free incense. Incense comes from the Latin *incensum*, meaning 'to burn'. The Arabic word for Frankincense, 'luban', derives from 'lbn', the root word for dairy products like yoghurt. It refers to the brilliant white colour of the resin immediately after scoring a Frankincense tree to obtain the resin. The resin is also known as *olibanum*. It derives from Latin through the Greek *libanos*, and originating from the Arabic word for Frankincense, *luban*. Frankincense can refer to the tree and the resin in Arabic and English.

Frankincense is a species within the plant genus *Boswellia* that was given its scientific name commemorating Dr John

Boswell, AD 1710-1780, the President of the Royal College of Physicians in Edinburgh from AD 1770-72; Boswell was uncle to the biographer James Boswell.

*Frankincense trees and Jabal Dhofar*

The Frankincense species found in Oman has had a confusing naming process. It was given its species name *'sacra'* from the Latin meaning sacred in 1867 by Friedrich August Flückiger, the Swiss botanist. Later, in 1870, Dr George Birdwood, who had been superintendent of the Agri-Horticultural Society's gardens in Bombay, named it *Boswellia carteri* after Dr H.J. Carter, the surgeon on a British exploration ship Palinurus. This ship was influential in the European re-discovery of Al Balid. Dr Carter incorrectly thought it was the same species that grows in India and named it *Boswellia serrata* in 1846. People were confused about what species were found in Oman due to this slightly convoluted naming history. Today, experts have firmly established *Boswellia sacra* as the name for the only *Boswellia* species that grows in Oman.

IN OMAN, THE FRANKINCENSE TREE GROWS IN MUCH OF the great crescent of mountains in Dhofar that extend from Ash Shuwaymiyyah 180 km to the east of Salalah and Dalkut 100 km to Salalah's west, then continuing onto the area of Al Fatk in Yemen 160km west from Salalah. These mountains, in Oman - Jabal Dhofar, are principally Limestone, with some intrusions of igneous rock in the eastern region. Frankincense trees grow directly into both types of rock. Behind Salalah, the mountains rise steeply from a narrow coastal plain that is only 15km wide. The mountains typically undulate between 700-1000 meters high, rising in the east beyond Mirbat to 1700 meters. The range, including the northern foothills, is some 60-120km between the coast and the desert in the north. Deep *wadis* (valleys) cut into the mountains. The *wadis* may make the short journey south into the Arabian Sea or the longer journey north into the desiccated Rub Al Khali, where any flash flood water sinks into the water table or evaporates under the extreme Arabian sun.

The crescent shape and height of the Dhofar Mountains creates a natural trap for the Monsoon wind, which sweeps from the African coast towards Asia from June through September. In Dhofar, this period is known as the Khareef الخريف. The Monsoon builds in intensity as the rising heat over Arabia and Asia drags in cooler, moist air from over the ocean. The air drag also pulls up cooler water from the ocean, which drops the air temperature further. As the air flows over the mountain barrier, the additional drop in temperature caused by the increase in elevation means that the cool air can no longer retain the water vapour. Water droplets form, creating towering Cumulonimbus cloudbanks over the mountains. On the mountain slopes facing the sea, the clouds frequently reach ground level, and the water condenses onto the vegetation, allowing a seasonal cloud forest to form. To the north, the dry desert air sucks the moisture from the clouds so that they disappear above the northern foothills.

These mountains are the backbone of the Land of Frankincense, a region of tremendous geography with a lengthy history and unique culture. At its heart is the Frankincense tree.

THE FRANKINCENSE TREE IS NOT LARGE, REACHING around five metres high. It grows from a single or several short trunks with an open-branched, often cone-shaped appearance. Fine pale grey hair covers the younger branches. Older Frankincense trees exhibit khaki-coloured bark that peels away from the wood, giving the appearance of strips of antiquated papyrus hanging from the trunk and creating a marvellous rustling sound in a breeze. Almost hidden by the fissured bark on mature trees Ants, possibly *Trichomyrmex mayri* or *Crematogaster sp*, may protect the tree from destructive beetles & larvae such as Long-horned Beetle *Neoplocaederus atlanticus* and *Sphenoptera chalcichroa*. The Ants may also reduce browsing by livestock. The new growth of bright, fresh, harlequin green leaves is considered good fodder for livestock and camels, which readily browse the trees. The older leaves on mature trees are a dark bottle green colour, approximately ten cm long and up to three cm wide. They are made up of paired leaflets, giving a tooth-like appearance to each leaf edge.

*Frankincense Flowers & Seed Pod with Apis florea bee*

Frankincense blossoms are small and delicately creamy yellow with five petals and have both stamens and pistils. Two or three dozen flowers cluster along a stalk up to 12 cm long and will bloom over a few weeks. The flowering period is usually from March to May, just before the summer Monsoon. However, some trees flower in October and November. Despite their small size, the flowers attract many insect pollinators, including butterflies, wasps, ants, the nomadic Little Bee *Apis florea* and the Honeybee *Apis mellifera jemenitica*. During the tree's flowering period, beekeepers from the region relocate their hives into areas with a concentration of Frankincense trees, so that a once-a-year production of Frankincense honey is made. After pollination, the flower's central disc turns a rich orange as the petals fall away and the developing pistil changes from green to a rich brown fruit (drupe). The plant produces tiny seed capsules, which have slight wings to facilitate dispersal by wind and water in the *wadis* where it grows.

Frankincense resin naturally exudes from the tree, especially if the tree is injured. Still, for commercial purposes, the tree is tapped in a similar way to a Rubber Tree. The resin includes several chemicals, including *Alpha-pinene,* a compound that dilates the bronchi within the lung. The percentage of *Alpha-pinene* within the resin varies according to the region where the tree grows, with a high concentration giving off an unpleasant odour. *Boswellic acid* is also found; it is a compound being investigated for its anti-cancer effectiveness, benefits to the liver, and help with asthmatics. An additional beneficiary compound is *Glucuronic acid*, which seems to reduce inflammation.

In most areas where the trees grow, the tapping season is during the period on either side of the Monsoon, as the mist impacts many aspects of the harvest, especially the perceived quality of the resin. Therefore, the tapping season starts in October, and May is the end of the season. June and July are the main harvest periods in areas unaffected by the Monsoon clouds. People believe that the resin tapped in hotter weather is superior to the one tapped in cooler weather.

*Cutting a Frankincense Tree's bark*

Frankincense trees can produce resin commercially when they are approximately ten years old, and tapping might continue production for seventy to eighty years. The tool used to tap the tree is called a *Managaf* and is a simple chisel with a broad, short metal blade and a wooden handle. The tapper makes shallow cuts in several places using the *Managaf*, which removes the outer papyrus-like bark and the young inner bark, often a green colour, revealing the orange cortex. Four or five centimetres wide and up to ten centimetres long, the cut is not usually very large.

*Frankincense Tree, Resin and* Managaf

Once made, a white, milky resin will flow almost immediately. If this is an initial cut, the Frankincense resin will be of little commercial value to the connoisseur; the subsequent three or four cuts, over perhaps several months, made in the same place will produce a more desirable quality. The resin is left to ooze out and remains on the tree, gradually becoming less liquid. After a week or more, the man returns to scrape it off into a container. It is then allowed to dry for a few more weeks, traditionally in the shelter of a cave, before being transported to market.

Describing the process, after an exploration of the region in 1928, Bertram Thomas, a British official in the Oman government, wrote, "The process is that the collectors – women as well as men – make a slight incision in the bark from which the sap exudes, and a week later they return to scrape off the dried resinous substance, pear-shaped and aromatic, and send it to the coast for export. In ancient times, the Egyptians used this magical produce in rituals. It still serves a religious purpose but is not sent east to the temples of India".

As with all natural products, Frankincense resin has many different qualities. In the 14th century AD, Chinese merchants classified it into 13 grades, including the finest quality, which was called by the very evocative name *ti-ju* (dripping milk), through to the less desirable *shui-shi-hei-ta* (water damaged – following its long sea voyage to China) and finally *chan-mo* (powder - which is the dust after sorting the grades). In the past, the mountain tribes of Dhofar recognised 9 qualities and types. Like connoisseurs of natural products worldwide, buyers from Dhofar might even ask where the tree grew before they bought the resin.

∾

## MEDICINE

Traditional medicinal uses merge into modern treatment.

Though ceremonies and rites may have consumed the most significant quantity of Frankincense resin, it was also highly valued medicinally. Frankincense resin was thought to enhance general well-being and used for various specific medical treatments. The 'Ebers Papyrus', written in Egypt in c 1550 BC, recommended Frankincense resin and cumin to treat a tooth "which gnaws against and opens the flesh". It also suggests Frankincense for throat and larynx infections, and to stop asthma, bleeding, phlegm and vomiting.

The father of medicine, Hippocrates, who was born in 460 BC, recommended Frankincense to treat burns, ulcers, sores and as an emollient. Aulus Cornelius Celsus (died 50AD), the Roman medicinal writer, recorded in his book, De Medicina, various treatments that included Frankincense in the mix - strengthening the voice, treatment of burns, suppressing bleeding, healing a wound, drawing out pus, cleaning wounds, treat dropsy, pleurisy, incipient absces, heal ulcers, treat vitiligo, heal various issues in the eye - more interestingly a haemorrhage from the membrane covering the brain, and finally - relaxing constrictions.

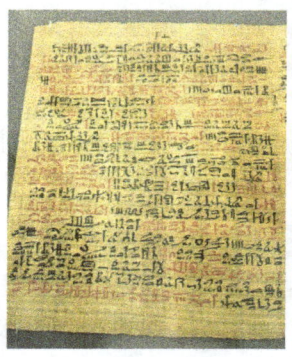

*Ebers Papyrus*

As if being considered a cure-all was not enough, the resin was also part of an antidote for poison. King Mithridates VI Eupator, who ruled Pontus in Anatolia from 120–63 BC, had his own acclaimed poison antidote, *Antidotum Mithridaticum*, a potion noted by Celsus. Included in the ingredients was Frankincense resin, and the king regularly consumed it. After his defeat during war against Rome in 63 BC, Mithridates tried to commit suicide by poisoning, having previously successfully tested the poison on his daughters. While they died quickly, he survived and instructed a soldier to kill him - *Antidotum Mithridaticum* apparently worked.

Celsus says that one of the Ptolemy rulers was given 'ambrosia' that included male Frankincense resin by the physician Zopyrus in the first century BC as part of his antidote to poisoning.

The use of Frankincense resin for medicinal purposes has continued into modern times, though not to resist poisons. The official Pharmacopeia of India, published in AD 1868, prescribed Frankincense resin to relieve chronic pulmonary afflictions. Pharmacopeia suggested a Frankincense ointment for ulcerations and boils.

In Oman, during much of the 20th century AD, traditional medicine continued to rely on Frankincense. People might use water infused with the bark as an antiseptic, or they might use powdered charcoal made from the bark. People used the resin to temporarily fill damaged teeth and reduce halitosis. Chewing the resin has been considered to strengthen the gums and teeth. If placed in a water bottle overnight, some pieces of resin will diffuse, and the water can be drunk in the morning. Some think this improves digestion. If the skin is inflamed or sore, a paste of bark was considered to have antiseptic qualities if applied onto the skin.

During pregnancy, women have used chewing bark for morning sickness. Later, during childbirth, burning Frankincense resin helped protect the mother and the newborn baby. Broken bones were set with a plaster made of softened gum, which would harden, held in place with bark, providing firm support while the bone healed.

∼

*Distillation of Frankincense Resin for Oil*

IN THE 21ST CENTURY AD, according to a team headed by Dr Mahmoud M. Suhail, *Boswellia sacra* essential oil is toxic to breast cancer cells in a tissue culture plate. A team from the University of Oklahoma also found the natural extract zeroed in and killed bladder cancer cells during laboratory tests. The German University of Tübingen observed an anti-inflammatory effect for rheumatoid arthritis. Traditional Chinese medical treatments use extracts from Frankincense resin to help a wide range of disorders, including ulcerated wounds.

People can distil Frankincense oil and use it for Aromatherapy with massage oils or place it in a vaporiser. People often consider Frankincense oil to have benefits that aid relaxation, reduce mental tension, improve the mood, and enhance breathing.

Today, as with any medicine or treatment, a patient's Doctor should always be consulted before any action is taken.

Harking back to Rome is the prestigious perfume producer Amouage, based in Muscat. Their men's and women's perfumes use Frankincense oils to create a unique and attractive fragrance.

*Amouage*

Perhaps today's most visible illustration of Frankincense, is a graphic rendering of Frankincense smoke – used as Oman Air's Logo.

TODAY, AS PRICES ARE NO LONGER SO PROHIBITIVE OR buyers are less discerning, there are only four usual classifications of resin, compared to those earlier 13 qualities of the Chinese. The finest is *Al Hojari*, harvested during the hottest season and named after the rugged region to the north of Jebel Samhan that is rarely touched by the moisture of the Monsoon. Individual pieces of *Al Hojari* Frankincense are large, well-formed, and almost drop-like with a translucent appearance and a flash of turquoise; this classification must be the 'dripping milk' of the Chinese merchants. Another grade is *Al Najdi*, named after the Najd or stony foothills on the desert side of the mountains. The Najd may have 'flash floods' and occasional storms brought about by the intense humidity build-up during the Monsoon. *Al Shazri*

variety is from the *wadi*-dissected region behind Jebel Qamar, which has a canopy of thick clouds above the mountains and high humidity during the monsoon season. The lowest quality is *Al Sahili*, which comes from the seasonally cloud-soaked coastal areas and can only be harvested during winter. Each classification varies in appearance, with the least expensive made up of smaller brown granules.

# CHAPTER 3
# HISTORY

**H**ISTORY
Over the millennia, the miasma of history and legend surrounding Frankincense have intertwined, with myth becoming fact and fact seeming almost mythical. Frankincense is one of the most famous gifts ever given, but today, although its name may still resonate, Frankincense's history is little known.

∽

ALMOST AT THE START OF RECORDED HISTORY, THE ancient Egyptians believed drops of Frankincense resin were tears from Horus, the Falcon god of the sky. In the Meidum Pyramid, one of the first pyramids ever built around 2550 BC, there is ancient graffiti in Hieratic script: "The heaven rains with fresh Frankincense and drops incense upon the roof of the temple of the Horus King Snefru", the king (ruled 2575 - 2551 BC) who completed the Bent Pyramid, Meidum Pyramid and Red Pyramid the impressive predecessors to the pyramids at Giza.

Egyptians may have ritually anointed a mummified body with the fragrant resins of Frankincense. They also used Myrrh, a similar resin from a tree *Commiphora myrrha* that also grows in southern Arabia. Like Frankincense, there are other species of *Commiphora*, some being poisonous. After mummification, a ceremony called the 'opening of the mouth' occurred. While reciting, "Receive the eye of Horus, may the scent reach you," they circled the mummy with smouldering Frankincense resin.

*Horus and Queen Nefatari – Valley of the Queens*

Queen Hatshepsut of Egypt sent an expedition of 5 ships

from Egypt to the Land of Punt (the southern end of the Red Sea) around 1493 BC. Amongst the products brought back to Luxor in Egypt were Frankincense resin, living tree specimens, and animals. It was considered an astounding triumph. "Never was anything like that brought to any king" – was the self-congratulatory inscription on Queen Hatshepsut's temple near the Valley of the Kings. It was the first successful importation of foreign trees. The remains of a claimed specimen is still in front of the temple.

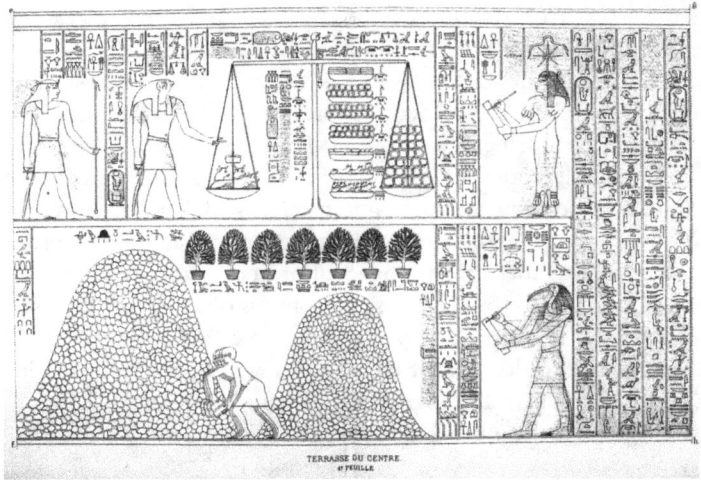

*Queen Hatshepsut – Punt Expedition (artist unknown)*

The Egyptians believed in a greater power for Frankincense resin than King Mithridates VI Eupator with his *Mithridatium antidotum* that could only prevent poisoning. The resin was part of the embalming process, enabling the body to be reunited with the soul and return to life after death. In the tomb of Tutankhamun, who died in 1323 BC, Howard Carter found four shaped Frankincense balls, created from Frankincense resin powder, to accompany the Pharaoh on his journey into the afterlife.

It was not only the ancient Egyptians who valued

Frankincense resin. Herodotus, the Greek who was born in the Turkish part of the Persian Empire, wrote around 430 BC that "the trees which bear the Frankincense (resin) are guarded by winged serpents (*Ophies Pteretoi* or *Ophies Hypopteroi*), small in size, and of varied colours, and vast numbers hang about every tree." Herodotus also said 1,000 talents weight (over 30 tons) of Frankincense resin was burnt during a festival in the temple of Marduk, the patron God of Babylon and prime amongst all Babylonian gods. He explained that the Arabs of the port city of Gaza delivered 1,000 talents of Frankincense yearly as a tribute to King Darius of Persia, 522-486 BC. These are more realistic reports of the resin's use to a modern reader.

Plutarch, the Greek writer who lived from AD 46-120, related that after Alexander the Great, 356-323 BC, conquered Gaza at the northern end of the Frankincense trade route in Palestine, Alexander sent 500 talents weight, (16 metric tons) of Frankincense resin and a hundred talents (3.3 metric tons) of Myrrh resin to Leonidas, his childhood tutor. Leonidas had seen a young Alexander throw a handful of Frankincense resin into a fire and told him to be more sparing in his offerings until he was master of the countries from which those "sweet gums" came. Alexander included a letter to Leonidas with his extravagant gift, "I have sent you an abundance of myrrh and Frankincense, that in future you may not be stingy to the gods".

*Phoenix (in author's imagination)*

Despite the Greek and Roman world venturing into Frankincense resin-producing areas, the resin still held an extraordinary mystique. The poet Ovid, who died in AD 17, wrote that the legendary Phoenix bird fed on drops of Frankincense resin and lived for five hundred years. The bird would then build a funeral byre on top of a Date Palm, and a young Phoenix would emerge from its own body. After gaining strength, the young bird would carry its parent's body to the sun temple in Heliopolis, Egypt.

Homer highlighted the use of Frankincense in Greek times in the Iliad, written around 700 BC, when Achilles says, "the Gods can be reconciled to man by the burning of Frankincense". From around the same period, Hesiod states that the Gods can be appeased with libations and incense.

The Christian Bible contains many references to Frankincense resin, a sign of its fame and use in the Levant during the time before the Roman occupation of the region. In the Song of Solomon 4:6, "Until the cool of the day when the shadows flee away, I will go my way to the mountain of Myrrh and to the hill of Frankincense". In Isaiah 60:6, "A multitude of camels will cover you, the young camels of Midian and Ephah; All those from Sheba will come; they will bring gold and Frankincense and bear good news of the praises of the Lord".

The most profuse use and demand for Frankincense resin eventually came in Rome. The women of Rome gave such vast amounts of Frankincense resin for the funeral of the Roman ruler Sulla in 78 BC that they carried it on 210 litters. Ovid, the Roman poet 43 BC-AD 17, described the other god's grief if Jupiter had caused mankind to perish as "who would offer Frankincense at the altars", would no longer make offerings to them. This use of Frankincense as an offering increased during the reign of Augustus 27 BC-AD 14, as Senators poured a libation of wine and burnt Frankincense resin before meetings.

Trade from Arabia and India principally used Western Arabia and the Red Sea route, rather than The Gulf. This is because for much of the period when Rome was at it peak, an opposing Empire in Persia restricted use of The Gulf and overland routes through Mesopotamia. The Parthians, from 248BC, were succeeded by the Sasanians in AD224. The Sasanians occupied the Levant and Egypt from the Byzantines for a decade, after 619. The area was again taken from Byzantine as The Levant was taken in 637 and Egypt in 641 by the Muslim army of the Caliph Umar.

*Augustus as a Pharoah offering incense - Temple of Kalabsha Egypt*

HIGH DEMAND FOR Frankincense resin in Rome created a thriving retail trade in the product. Horace, writing in the first century BC, explained that shops on the Vicus Tuscus (now Via di San Teodoro) north of the Circus Maximus were the focus of the trade. These shops represented the terminus of the Frankincense trail that originated in Dhofar.

*Via di San Teodoro*

Apart from the economic benefits for the people living at either end of the Frankincense trail, the inhabitants of towns along the route were beneficiaries. They levied taxes on caravans at town gates; town traders might provide accommodation, food, animal fodder and water, while powerful tribes charged fees for safe passage within their territory.

The trail was not a single linear path between Dhofar and Rome, as there were options along most of its route. Nevertheless, over the centuries, many towns formed critical elements of the Frankincense Trail on the western side of Arabia.

These include Shibam, Shabwah, Tumna, Marib, and Qarnaw in modern Yemen; and Najran, Tabala (now Bishah), Yathrib (now Medinah), Hijra (now Hegra / previously usually called Madain Saleh) in today's Saudi Arabia. Petra and the port city of Gaza were in the final stages before the merchandise was sent by sea to Rome.

The entire route might have been 4,000km, taking up to 40 days, at a walking pace for both man and Camel. Shabwah was the critical hub for various routes and guarded the exit from the vital route through Wadi Hadhramaut. The sea route between Dhofar and Rome became part of the more extended Rome-to-India trade. However, sea trade offered minimal scheduling advantage, as when the main harvest was available for transport to the northwest and Rome, the Monsoon wind was blowing towards the northeast. Despite this lack of significant time benefit, sea transportation became an important trade component.

26  LAND OF FRANKINCENSE

*Shibam Yemen*

Rome tried over the years to control the Frankincense trade. The most notable event was when Roman Emperor Augustus sent Aelius Gallus, the governor of Egypt, into Arabia Felix, southern Arabia, in AD 25. He led an army of 10,000 men supported by 1,500 North Arabian auxiliaries. With guidance from a Nabataean man from North Arabia, the outward journey took six months, more than double the time a trade caravan of laden Camels would take. Finally, they reached

'Marsiaba', which was probably modern Marib in Yemen, or Al Abr 200km farther northeast, and besieged the town for six days.

*Tombs, Jabal Ahmar, Hegra - Saudi Arabia*

Disease and lack of food forced Aelius Gallus to return to Egypt, having lost a substantial part of his army. Aelius Gallus made the return journey in 60 days and blamed his guide for deliberate deceit during the outward journey. Rome never attempted the conquest of this area again. However, they controlled the northern part of the Frankincense route into Rome when, in AD 106, the Roman Emperor Trajan occupied Petra in Jordan. This brough the Roman Empires Arabian border south to Hegra.

Rome and the Himyaritic kingdom established diplomatic relations following that disastrous military campaign. The Periplus of the Erythraean Sea, is a written description of marine travel in the Arabian Sea region around the 1$^{st}$ Century AD, the author states, "There is Saphar, the metropolis, in which lives Charibael, lawful king of two tribes, the Homerites and those living next to them, called the Sabaites; through continual embassies and gifts, he is a friend of the Emperors" (of Rome).

The Homerites are the Himyarites and Sabaites the Sabaeans, both states in Yemen.

*Ad Deir - Petra the Nabataean capital*

It fell to the Roman Emperor Nero to show how power and Frankincense were entwined. Pliny the Elder (alive AD 23 – 79) wrote that at the funeral of Nero's remarkable wife, Poppea in AD 65, an entire year's production of Frankincense resin was burned. During Nero's rule, the Great Fire of Rome started in shops dealing in flammable material near the Circus Maximus. What better flammable material than Frankincense.

Nigel Groom, who wrote about Frankincense and its trade, estimates that during the period Pliny wrote about, up to 10,000 camels would carry Frankincense resin annually to ports such as Gaza for onward shipment to Rome. Pliny also detailed the retail value of Frankincense resin in Rome, along with other exotic imports. Pepper cost up to 15 Denarii per pound, Myrrh resin up to 16 Denarii per pound and best Frankincense resin 6 Denarii per pound, with the poorest quality at 3 Denarii. The myth that Frankincense resin was as valuable as Gold is debunked by the fact that it only cost around 15% of Gold's price. Emperor

Augustus had fixed Gold at 42 gold aureus (1050 Denarii) per pound.

*Camels & Goats Hair Tent*

Groom estimates that the value of the Frankincense trade into Rome was 9,900,000 Denarii, and those 10,000 Camels may have carried up to 1500 British tons, in total, or around 360 pounds (163 kilo) each. So although weight for weight, the value was not as great as Gold, the vast volume was an economic drain on Rome, as was the import of other spices, all of which were paid for in precious metal as Rome's exported goods had little appeal in the Land of Frankincense.

The trade in Frankincense resin after Pliny's time significantly increased, with the precious cargo increasingly being carried by sea.

Today, the most famous presentation of Frankincense resin followed the birth of Jesus. In the Bible, Matthew 2, "After Jesus was born in Bethlehem in Judea, during the time of King Herod, Magi from the east came to Jerusalem"..." they saw the child with his mother Mary, and they bowed down and worshipped him. Then they opened their treasures and presented him with gifts of Gold, Frankincense and Myrrh". The Persian historian

Muhammad ibn Jarir Al Tabari, writing in the 9th century AD, says that Wahb ibn Munabbih, who was born in cAD 654, wrote that three Kings travelled to search for Jesus "bearing Gold and Myrrh and Frankincense".

*Three Magi presents their gifts - Sant Apollinare - Chester M. Wood*

Marco Polo documented these Magi, a religious Zoroastrian caste in Persia, and mentioned that there is a city called Saba (Saveh) from where the three Magi originated. They came to adore Christ in Bethlehem.

King Shammar Yuharish of the Yemeni Kingdom of Himyar conquered the Hadhramaut in about AD 300. Samharam may have been the most easterly settlement under Himyar. Improved security in the region allowed growth in the trade. The increase in trade and the established relationship with Rome prompted Himyar to receive Roman embassies. These organised the building of churches for Roman merchants in Himyar's trade towns as Christianity gradually became adopted in the Empire.

In AD 380 Emperor Theodosius established Christianity as the official religion in the Roman Empire. Making sacrifices or giving offerings, including incense, to pagan gods were prohibited in 381. The prohibition was increased through to 395, and the death of Theodosius, the last Emperor of a unified Empire. His son Arcadius became the Emperor of Byzantine, (Eastern Rome) and in 399 he ordered that all pagan temples were to be demolished. This created adverse market conditions for Frankincense in Rome and later its successor in Byzantine.

Despite the edicts of Emperors Theodosius & Arcadius, Christian Churches still use incense today.

Richer ones may use Frankincense resin in their rituals. Hopefully, they use sacred *Boswellia sacra*. This use of incense is particularly the case in Catholic and Orthodox churches where a censer called a Thurible censes worshipers or objects. One of the most remarkable examples can be found in Santiago de Compostela Cathedral in Spain, where several men are needed to

*Thurible*

swing a gigantic Thurible (*Botafumeiro*) using chains. In Judaism, Moses received instructions from God to use incense in ceremonies at the Tabernacle. Hindu Temples and other Asian religions also use incense, though not normally Frankincense.

THE USE OF FRANKINCENSE IN OMAN TODAY IS STEEPED in history yet is still part of everyday life.

Today, most people in Oman buy Frankincense resin to use as incense. Omanis continue to use specially made incense burners called *Majmar,* just like in historic times. There are two standard core designs in Oman, both made from clay. Potters in northern Oman make the *Majmar* on a potter's wheel, while women in the region around Mirbat in Dhofar fashion the *Majmar* design from slabs of clay. Elegant burners made from silver and other metals appeal to more affluent people. The silver styling has influenced the iconic monument overlooking Sultan Qaboos Port in Muscat, Electronically heated burners that can be plugged into a car's cigarette lighter are also used by the person on the move.

So the resin does not burn or create a flame, an external heat source is used to heat it. Using a traditional pottery burner, a disc of charcoal is placed in it, with a few granules of Frankincense resin on top of the disc.

Majmar made using a slab method of creation - Mirbat Dhofar

SINCE THE RESIN WILL MELT OVER ANY *MAJMAR'S* surface, aluminium foil placed below the charcoal & resin will keep the *Majmar* in good condition. The charcoal is set to smoulder using the flame from a cigarette lighter, or similar item, and the resin placed on the disc will give off smoke. In social gatherings in Oman, hosts often pass around a *Majmar* with some smoking Frankincense resin and hold it in front of each guest. The guest can then use both hands to waft the smoke towards them so that the fragrant smoke will perfume themselves.

This aromatic smoke from Frankincense resin can also fragrance clothing. To fragrance clothing, people use a specially made stand called a *Mabkharah*. The *Mabkharah* is usually a pyramid shape with legs that are 50-70cm high, and it has a mesh between its legs on which clothes are draped. A *Majmar* is placed inside the stand so that the aroma of the rising smoke adds its scent to the fabric, and as an added advantage, it drives off insects.

In Oman, some believe the aromatic smoke from Frankincense resin will ward off evil spirits. If a person is considered under a malevolent influence, Frankincense is heated and, within a ceremony, the sprits are driven away by the holy smoke. Some people use Frankincense smoke to waft inside a new vehicle, to help protect both vehicle and its occupants from danger, including accidents - almost harking back to its historic protective properties.

All parts of the *Boswellia sacra* tree have a traditional use. Before it completely hardens, one can chew the resin like chewing gum. Macerating and simmering the bark in water infuses the water with a rich red-brown ochre dye, which can then dye clothes or leather. The soot from Frankincense smoke is used as a *kohl*, an eye cosmetic, which is believed to help keep eye infections away and reduce the reflection of sunlight, quite apart from giving the eye Jack Sparrow or Sophia Loren looks.

*Incensing the Tomb of the Prophet Job - Salalah*

Mabkharahs *in an Omani Suq*

# CHAPTER 4
# WADI DAWKAH UNESCO SITE

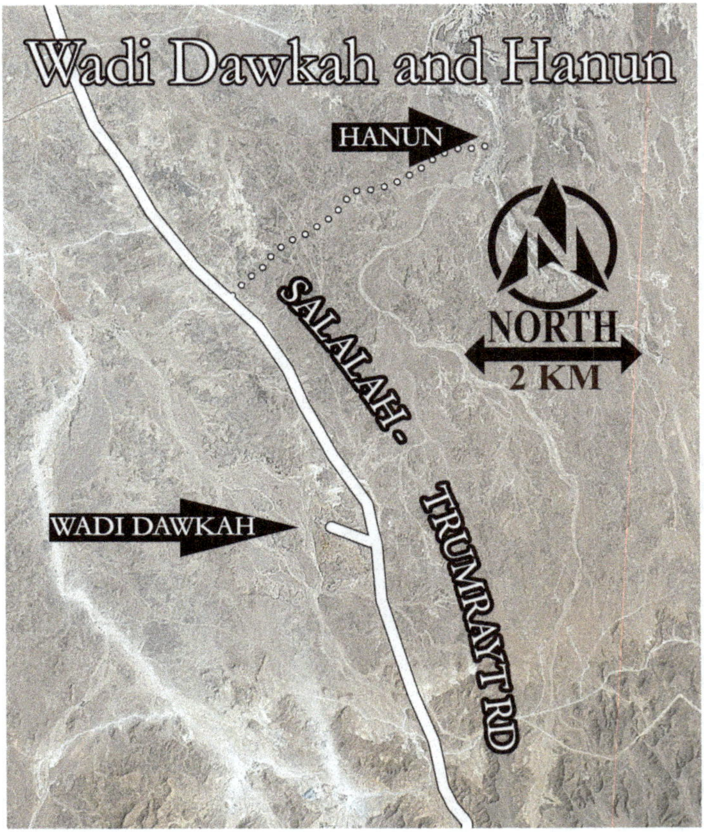

![Map of Wadi Dawkah and Hanun area showing Salalah-Trumrayt Rd, with arrows pointing to Hanun and Wadi Dawkah, scale 2 KM]

## Wadi Dawkah UNESCO Site
وادي دوكة

A natural, pre-historic landscape is the site of Dhofar's most numerous concentration of Frankincense trees.

NEAR THE SMALL VILLAGE OF QAYRUN HAYRITI, ON the north-facing slopes of the Dhofar Mountains that overlook Salalah, is the source of the great Wadi Dawkah. The *wadi* descends north from 830 meters above the sea and gradually fans out as it reaches the desert plateau, 450 meters below its source. Here, it becomes less distinct until the sands of the Rub Al Khali sweep over it after a journey of over 165 km. As the Monsoon is now less powerful than before, surface water flow is unusual in today's Wadi Dawkah.

However, there is still a hidden underground water flow, which fodder farms, on the desert's edge, use. Seen from the air, vast green circles dot the landscape in the northern area of Wadi Dawkah. These are typically Rhodes Grass fields, some may be Wheat, irrigated by pivot arms up to four hundred metres long. Water pumped up from below the surface feeds the pivot arms, spraying it onto the crops, maintaining rapid crop growth under the intense desert sun. The grass is cut three or four times a year for fodder, which is then sun-dried (a quick process in the desert), bailed and loaded onto trucks. Trucks deliver the feed to farmers in the mountains. They follow the course of Wadi Dawkah back up to Qayrun Hayriti and farther south.

*Pivot Field and Sprinkler*

A natural terrace on the edge of Wadi Dawkah, some six km north of Qayrun Hayriti, bears the remains of some of Dhofar's more enigmatic ancient monuments, 'Triliths'.

A former British official in Oman, Bertram Thomas, a Minister to Sultan Said bin Taimur, saw Triliths when he became the first European to travel from Salalah through the Rub' Al Khali to Qatar in 1930. He used the term Trilith and noted inscriptions on some, in what is now called South Arabian script.

During his journeys through Oman after 1945, Wilfred Thesiger described them as Trilithons. He observed them in groups of three to fifteen, with each group consisting of three stone slabs approximately two feet high. These slabs stood on end and leaned against each other, forming a triangle at their base.

Considering their purpose, Thesiger continued, "Bertram Thomas thought Trilithons marked the sites of graves, but I frequently found them erected above solid rock. I think they may have been commemorative".

*Triliths Wadi Dawkah*

Archaeologists date the Triliths to between the 2nd century BC and 4th century AD. This is broadly the period of the maximum trade in Frankincense. Archaeologists find Triliths from the Hadramaut, through Dhofar north of the Dhofar Mountains, and up the east coast of Oman to around Bani Bu Ali. Their purpose remains to be determined.

The Wadi Dawkah UNESCO World Heritage Site is five km

downstream from the Triliths. Like all the great north-facing *wadis* of Dhofar, Wadi Dawkah cuts through Tertiary Limestone (2.6-66 m years ago) rock. Water flooding scours the rock surface clean, maintaining the *wadi's* creamy white surface, while above the floods, a surface of dark lichen may coat the rock.

The UNESCO selection committee chose Wadi Dawkah as the site representing the location of Frankincense resin harvesting in ancient times, as it is in an intact natural landscape, which offers ease of access due to its proximity to a major road. The almost square boundary of the site covers an area of eight square km, where the *wadi* has spread and is dissected by isolated low mesas.

*Chert & Flint Core reduction area on a Mesa in Wadi Dawkah*

Scattered on the surface of several of these mesas are chert and flint. Near the Wadi Dawkah site, Dr Jeffery Rose, an archaeologist specialising in human migration through Southern

Arabia, made a small nine-square-metre excavation and found chert/flint that ancient man had crafted. Just above the layer of flint chippings was a tell-tale sign of the ancient climate in Wadi Dawkah: a shell from a small land snail *Euryptyxis latireflexa* that was AMS radiocarbon dated to c10,430 years ago. The presence of the snail gives a very different picture of the past environment of Wadi Dawkah compared to today's, as the snail's usual habitat is dense grassland. The snail's preferred habitat can be found in areas of Dhofar today, such as the lake-filled Wadi Darbat near Khawr Rawri.

The vegetation at the Wadi Dawkah site is dominated by Frankincense trees, which are scattered over about five square km. Several hundred trees grow naturally within the *wadi*, mainly to the east of the largest mesa. Though protected in the Wadi Dawkah site, Frankincense trees are under pressure elsewhere in Dhofar. Dr Mohsin Al Amri, an expert in Frankincense, has worked on a project to identify major causes for this. He considers over-tapping of the tree's resin, over-grazing by livestock, mining projects and the construction of roads to be among the key elements. As a result, the government of Oman is cultivating Frankincense trees at several sites, including Wadi Dawkah, where they have planted around 5,000 trees and are providing water through drip-feed irrigation.

*Land Snails - Wadi Darbat*

The regimented lines of newly planted trees are less striking than the larger, ancient ones just outside the fenced area. These stretch north beyond the Mesa, opposite the planted area, for some 2 kilometres.

∾

## Visiting Wadi Dawkah GPS 17.338810, 54.076603

The site is a 44km drive north of central Salalah and 32km south of Thumrayt on the west of the main road. Wadi Dawkah is best visited when driving south to Salalah. A junction, when driving north, allows a turn from the Dual Carriageway, though returning to this north carriageway requires an additional drive south to find another turn. This site, though not a must-see as there are Frankincense Trees in Al Balid & west of Mughsayl in more dramatic scenery, adds interest if driving to visit Ash Shisr and the Empty Quarter.

*Ancient Frankincense Trees & Monsoon Clouds Wadi Dawkah*

# CHAPTER 5
# HANUN

# Hanun
حنون

Hanun is an ancient storage area for Frankincense resin overlooking Wadi Rabkut, one of the north-flowing *wadis* of Dhofar.

∾

Surrounding Hanun is a geology of Tertiary Limestone (2.6-66 m years ago). The newly exposed Limestone has a creamy colour compared to rock whose surface has not been stripped by weathering, exfoliation, or rock fall. This effect is evident on the cliffs of Wadi Rabkut. Saxicolous lichens cover the surface that has been eroded less recently, creating a dark, crumbly overlay on the older exposed areas. Along the course of Wadi Rabkut, there is some surface water flow with occasional pools close to Hanun. As with many of the *wadis* that flow north from the Dhofar mountains, there are a few trees at the base of the *wadi*, including Acacia, Date Palm and a some Frankincense trees farther south. On the *wadi's* cliff edge, opposite the site of Hanun, slightly to its north, is the most impressive location for Dhofar's Triliths. Triliths are found from near Bani bu Ali, in northern Oman, south through Dhofar into southern Yemen. In Oman, especially in Dhofar, they are mainly on the desert side of the mountains, and invariably, they are placed directly on solid rock, with each row having an odd number of the upright grouping.

The dating of Triliths throughout Oman is between the 2$^{nd}$ century BC and 4$^{th}$ century AD. Though the purpose is unknown, they may be some form of ceremonial site.

Hanun served as a storage area within the overland Frankincense resin trade route. Wendell Phillips described 'nine long narrow storage bins' in 1960 and considered the site to be seasonal in use during the harvest season. Unfortunately, the limited excavations at Hanun have had little information about them published. The area's excavations have located stone tools of the Palaeolithic period, older than 11,650 BC. An inscription found here refers to 'Sakalan'. This is the name used around the period that Samharam flourished for the entire region.

Triliths above Wadi Rabkut

Hanun is believed to be a 'satellite' of Samharam and was

established during the third century BC. Its floor layout is comparable to the Frankincense storerooms at Samharam: a central corridor and long rooms leading off it, and one can imagine that the access was from an upper part of the wall or the roof, as is assumed to be the case in Samharam.

*Hanun Frankincense Storage Rooms*

**VISITING HANUN 17.382000, 54.104000**

Hanun is most easily reached when travelling north from Salalah towards Thumrayt. The site access is around 51km north of central Salalah's Clock Tower and 25km south of Thumrayt on the northbound carriageway of the main road from Salalah. An exit (17.367119, 54.069755) leads towards the east from the main road. This exit is about 3.5km after the Wadi Dawkah turn and 5km south of the turn to a waste disposal area. A rough track leads east from the main road for 5km towards the impressive Wadi Rabkut. The track is used for access to a weather station next to the archaeological site, and is marked by oil drums. Before the sheer cliff of the *wadi*, look to the left for the modern wall surrounding Hanun - and of course stop and park well before the cliff. The track crosses several small gullies, and flash flood damage may damage the route slightly; there are several alternative tracks even on this short journey. When crossing the gullies, a 4x4 vehicle gives good ground clearance and extra traction. Hanun itself is small, however the Wadi Rabkut and the Triliths add to the appeal. It can make a good addition to a visit to Wadi Dawkah, Ubar and the more distant Empty Quarter.

# CHAPTER 6
# ASH SHISR
# UNESCO SITE

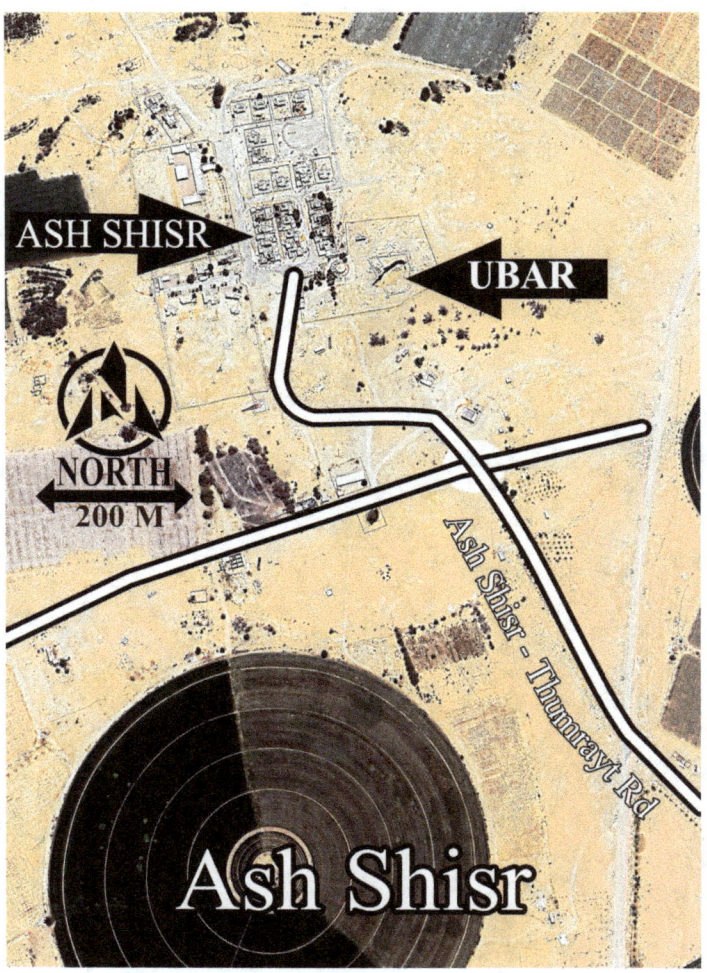

# Ash Shisr UNESCO Site
الشصر

Ash Shisr is the location of Ubar, the fabled town found after a legendary search. Today the site is given the name Wabar, but as Ubar is the variant most closely associated with the site, I have used that.

## ASH SHISR UNESCO SITE

OVER 140 KILOMETRES, AS THE EAGLE FLIES, FROM THE beaches of Salalah, Ash Shisr is in the middle of nowhere and on the edge of nothing, the Empty Quarter (Rub Al Khali). This desert stretches west from Ash Shisr for over 900 km towards Najran in Saudi Arabia and north for over 600 km to the Abu Dhabi island of Sir Bani Yas. Wilfred Thesiger described his impression of its dunes in his book Arabian Sands: "It seemed fantastic that this great rampart which shut out half the sky could be made of windblown sand".

THE HIJAZ MOUNTAINS, WHICH EXTEND DOWN THE length of the Red Sea coast of the Arabian Peninsula and the Dhofar Mountains (and their extension west into Yemen) along the coast of the Arabian Sea, create a rain shadow over much of the Arabian Peninsula. This shadow results in a desert that is desiccated even when compared to other deserts, giving rise to its name. Rising from the desert floor, the dunes of the Empty Quarter can reach an extraordinary height of 180 metres, their sides always on the verge of an avalanche, making walking here arduous and time-consuming.

Separating Ash Shisr from the main desert sands is Wadi Ghadun. The seemingly immobile yet persistently advancing dunes only a few kilometres from Ash Shisr are subsuming this ancient fossil river. The geology here is Limestone of the Hadhramaut Group, lower Eocene Rus formation (56 million to 48 million years ago). The Hadhramaut Group is a crucial water aquifer, and the Wadi Ghadun comes from a spread of dendritic tributaries 70km in breadth centred on Ayoun in the Dhofar Mountains south of Ash Shisr. From Ayoun to its final confluence, some 60 km north of Ash Shisr, the flow of water that could flood along its course was substantial. This historic flow created underground fossil water, and the age of the water, depending on its underground location, is between 200,000 and 550,000 years old.

*Rub Al Khali Desert*

This water, forming the aquifer, gave Ash Shisr its importance. Camel caravans leaving the *wadis* of the Dhofar Mountains found Ash Shisr provided the last good water for hundreds of kilometres. Some caravans would then travel west, into Yemeni towns like Shibam and north to the markets of the Mediterranean beyond. Some might leave Shisr and go north, to the oasis at Yabrin some 700km away and the wealthy markets of Iraq beyond that.

Naturally, with the lack of rainfall, there is little plant life; Acacia is the most obvious. Animals in the sands include the Sandcat, *Felis margarita*, Arabian toad-headed agama, *Phrynocephalus arabicus* and the mildly poisonous Sand Snake, *Psammophis schokari*. The plains east of Ash Shisr are probably still home to the Honey Badger, *Mellivora capensis*, with lizards including Dhab, *Uromastyx thomasi* (named after Bertram Thomas) and possibly fatal snakes including Burton's carpet viper, *Echis coloratus*. Birdlife is equally sparse, however Spotted Sandgrouse, *Pterocles senegallus*, & Crowned Sandgrouse, *Pterocles coronatus*, breed in the area. These birds use water sources many kilometres away, including at Hashman, a 70km drive northwest.

*Uromastyx thomasi*

Using the fossil water aquifer are 'centre pivot fields' and occasional 'linear fields', established at Ash Shisr in the year 2,000. These pivot fields are circular fields where a hollow metal arm rotates on a central pivot that feeds water from a borehole, drawing up water from the aquifer. The linear fields have a metal arm that moves up and down each field in a linear progression along the field.

Both systems spray water from their overhead arms onto the soil or crops below. Most of these fields in the Ash Shisr area provide fodder for Cattle and, to a lesser extent, for Camels and Goats/Sheep in the Dhofar Mountains.

The people of antiquity most closely associated with the fabled town of Ubar are the people of Ad, who inhabited southern Arabia before Islam. Many people believe their descendants are some of the tribes still living in Dhofar. In several chapters, the Quran describes the town, which is associated with Ubar and its people. "They denied the revelations of God and disobeyed His messenger, Hud, and did the bidding of every rebellious reprobate". The Quran describes their fate in Chapter 69, The Inevitable. "As for Ad, they were annihilated by a persistent, violent storm. He unleashed it upon them for seven nights and eight days, violently. You could see the people tossed around like decayed palm trunks. Can you find any trace of them?" The town disappeared, although it lived on in the memory of the region's inhabitants. Hud, the messenger to Ad, is said to have survived the storm, and today, there is a mausoleum hidden in a shallow valley, high in the Dhofar mountains, that is inscribed as Hud's (Hood's) burial place. Many of the explorers of the vast Arabian Desert have also become part of the site's history.

Bertram Thomas was the first European to cross the Rub Al Khali in 1930, guided by Bedouins from the tribes living in the region around Ash Shisr. He recounted their reaction as they crossed a track in the southern Empty Quarter, "Look, Sahib, they cried, there is the road to Ubar. Ubar? I wondered. It was a great city, our fathers have told us, that existed of old; a city rich in treasure, with date gardens and a fort of red silver".

Harry St. John Philby, who counted the conqueror of Saudi Arabia, King AbdulAziz, as a friend, searched for Ubar through the northern Empty Quarter in 1932. He described how his search came to its climax with a shout from one of his guides: "Look! exclaimed Ali suddenly, and I had my first glimpse of Wabar, a low thin line of ruins riding upon a wave of the yellow sands ... I looked down not upon the ruins of an ancient city but into the mouth of a volcano". This mouth of a volcano was a second location where local legend placed Ubar.

Wilfred Thesiger, the explorer of Oman in the late 1940s, learned of Ash Shisr's importance during his travels through the Empty Quarter with guides from the same families as those who had helped Thomas. "We watered at Ash Shisr, where the ruins of a crude stone fort on a rocky mound mark the position of the famous well, the only permanent water on the central steppes".

Wendell Phillips started the modern search for Ubar after he arrived in Dhofar in 1953 and explored the desert by truck. In his book Unknown Oman, he describes meeting a Bedouin and

"When I asked him if he knew the location of Ubar he shouted into my ear, Only the devil knows".

*Tomb of Hud*

. . .

Two men were instrumental in the discovery of Ubar and its subsequent fame. Nicholas Clapp and Sir Ranulph Fiennes who recounts a conversation he had with a colleague, Nasran, while serving with the military in Oman during the late 1960s, "Nasran smiled, some say the finest city in all Arabia was Ubar, built like Paradise with pillars fashioned from gold. Will you take me there Nasran? I asked. Inshalla was his reply". In the ensuing twenty years, what started as a conversation by Fiennes grew into a quest to discover the lost city.

The British Army had seconded Fiennes to the Reconnaissance Platoon of Oman's Muscat Regiment and had extensive active service during the 1965-75 Dhofar military activities. This experience gave him connections that enabled him to gain the support of Sultan Qaboos, Oman's monarch, and arrange financing from Omani backers. As the expedition's logistics director, he literally drove the mission to a climax.

*Fort at Ubar*

INITIAL SEARCHES BY CLAPP WERE FROM THE COMFORT of library chairs: "On Ptolemy's map of Arabia, if anywhere, I should find Ubar. And sure enough, on most editions, the tribal name *"Iobaritae"*, Latin for "Ubarites", appears, more or less, where Bertram Thomas encountered his road to Ubar." Serendipity brought Fiennes and Clapp together in 1986 when Clapp edited the film of Fiennes's attempted circumpolar expedition. Over the ensuing years, with the help of NASA, who provided satellite images of the region, the exploration to search for Ubar inched towards reality.

The archaeological dig started at Ubar in December 1991. Under the headline "On the Trail From the Sky: Roads Point to a Lost City", the New York Times published an article on 5th February 1992. "Guided by ancient maps and sharp-eyed surveys from space, archaeologists and explorers have discovered a lost city deep in the sands of Arabia, and they are certain it is Ubar, the fabled entrepot of the rich Frankincense trade thousands of years ago". Despite the news, the dig would not be finished until 1994.

*Fort & collapsed Cave at Ubar*

The team discovered a fortified settlement with a citadel, and evidence points to the site being used since c 5000 BC. The archaeologist responsible for the excavations, Juris Zarins, believes the fort was built on an earlier settlement. Evidence suggests that though the site continued in use in the Early and Middle Islamic periods, it had lost its importance by the third century AD.

The settlement's wall is a distorted pentagon, with eight or more bastions on the walls, some of which would have served as living quarters. The citadel was in the northwest corner, and south of this is the principal gate facing west, the direction most camel caravans would have departed towards. Set along the length of the exterior walling were inward-facing cubicles about 2.5 meters in width; these are like the layout at Ayn Hamran.

By far the most important, indeed essential, part of the fort was the area where there is now a massive rock collapse. When they built the fort, they used the solid roof of a cave in this area, which had a water source below it. At an unknown date the cave roof collapsed, which destroyed not only the fort but also its role in trade routes. Caravans would no longer need to visit as there was no easy water access.

Behind the ancient fortification is a more modern whitewashed fort built in 1955, using stone from the original fort. Its prime purpose was the same as that of its older counterpart: to defend its vital resource, water, which until 2011 was mechanically pumped up to irrigate a nearby Date plantation. Another purpose was to establish an Oman government presence in the region.

The objects found at Ash Shisr have been eclectic: Neolithic spear points and arrowheads (8th-7th centuries BC), glass bracelet fragments (9th-16th centuries AD), Abbasid coins (8th-10th centuries AD) and, most intriguingly, part of a chess set (8th-10th centuries AD).

Juris Zarins stated, "It was a key site with regard to the trade that was coming and going along the edge of the great Empty Quarter. And it's one of those major sites with water. So, there was a lost city of Ubar and we did find it!"

## Visiting Ubar 18.254829, 53.647722

Ash Shisr is a 170km drive northwest of Salalah along well-maintained tarmac roads. Slightly north of Thumrayt, a rough track is marked. However, the easier route is after a 41.6km drive north of Thumrayt's roundabout, where a tarmacked road leading to the west is found at 17.954993, 54.015833. The fort is 52km west of this junction. Entry is by ticket with a charge for a non-resident of Oman, OMR3 (child OMR1). A visitor's Kiosk is at the entrance. Next to the area of Ubar is a small shop, which will benefit from your business.

Ash Shisr, which is easily overshadowed by Samharam and Al Balid, requires a long drive to reach. Most visitors combine it with Wadi Dawkah (you might add Hanun) and the Empty Quarter, for which two or more 4x4 vehicles are ideal.

The 24-hour Shell Petrol Station area in Thumrayt offers petrol, snacks, and restaurants. In Ash Shisr, a non-franchised petrol pump with a small, very simple place for food is just northwest of the village, on the rough road to Hashman. Do not neglect to take advantage of this petrol - if it has a supply; there is nothing else beyond here. It does run-out of petrol on occasions.

# CHAPTER 7
# ANDHUR

# Andhur
أنظور

Within the Dhofar Mountain's northern slope is Wadi Andhur, the location of the remote site of Andhur.

~

THE ARCHAEOLOGICAL SITE OF ANDHUR IS SET ON A mesa at the confluence of two *wadis*. Each of their meandering route travels down from the escarpment of Jabal Samhan for almost 100km northwards through the foothills to Andhur. The now combined *wadi* named Wadi Andhur continues north from Andhur before ultimately fanning out into the central Oman plain after an additional convoluted journey of some 200km. All of the northern wadis in Jabal Samhan form a dendritic pattern of water courses. Shale, Marl, and Limestone of the Middle Eocene 48 to 38 million years ago form the foothills; the higher mountains towards the south are Limestone formed towards the end of the Middle Eocene at 38 million years ago. Along the *wadi* is evidence of mining for Chert, a raw material for stone tools. Outside the bed of the *wadis*, these foothills are almost devoid of vegetation; the rain shadow of the mountains and browsing by livestock gives seedlings practically no chance of survival. Spring water and a high water table in the bed of the *wadi* result in standing water pools near the archaeological site. Descendants of cultivated Dates *Phoenix dactylifera* and Mazari Palm *Nannorrhops ritchiana*, along with Reed, *Phragmites australis*, populate the area around the pools. There is a scattering of Acacia, *Acacia tortilis* and *Acacia ehrenbergiana* in the *wadi* bed, with some Aloe, *Aloe dhufarensis*, on the hills.

Date Palms grow poorly in the wild and, as they are usually only cultivated, provide a good sign of a previous permanent settlement in an area. Though most parts of the Date Palm have a use, the Date fruit is its most valuable product.

The Mazari Palm is a valuable resource for rope making, fibre and basket work as the material is better suited to wetting than most other alternatives. Its small fruit, though not as valuable as that from Date Palms, is edible and can be stored for months after it is dried.

*Andhur at the confluence of its wadi and Frankincense Smoke Logo on Oman Air*

A number of Arabian Gazelle *Gazella Arabica* are found in

the area, along with feral Donkeys. The water and vegetation amidst the desolation made Andhur a magnet for travellers.

*Gazelle in Wadi Andhur*

Bertram Thomas traversed across Wadi Andhur, south of the Andhur archaeological site, in early 1928. He thought that the "scant vegetation must be sustained by dew". Thesiger noted the archaeological site, locally called Qarbti, whose "walls were built of cut stone set in mortar, and were half buried in rubble". He followed the *wadi* south, where there is more water, before ascending the mountains.

In 1960 Wendell Phillips wrote of his visit to Andhur "Our Power Wagons, after crossing the Qara range, were bounced and badly knocked about as we drove in a reverse direction, south-southeast, up the *wadi* floor over a thick cover of rounded pebbles, cobbles and loose Limestone boulders". Later he described "Here the stones of the masonry were cut and placed in a fashion reminiscent of the original masonry at Samharam and the identical lime mortar, as used in the gateway and square towers of Samharam, are clear indications that this building belongs to the same general period, first century BC – fourth century AD."

Arriving by helicopter in 1990, Ranulph Fiennes reached Andhur in his search for Ubar (which his team say they found at Ash Shisr). He described the ruins as 'no bigger than the smallest of English cottages'. The archaeologist Juris Zarins, who was with Fiennes, found Indian 'Red Polished Ware' pottery (dated to the first century BC –third century AD) at Andhur, similar to pottery found at Ash Shisr. Later, Zarins wrote the area may have been a focus of humans during the Bronze Age, if not earlier.

*Andhur's Mesa*

Today, the site is much as these explorers saw it, no excavations have taken place. After arriving at Andhur today and perhaps parking on the low hill opposite the mesa to its west, walking through the palms is a rewarding experience. It brings home how abundant the water and vegetation must have appeared to any person arriving on foot or Camel. The ascent up the mesa's slope is relatively easy, though a stick and suitable walking footwear is ideal and, as always, the descent is more difficult.

The fortification on top of this mesa provided security, visual surveillance, and protection from extreme flooding. Today, the limited remains of walling, using stone blocks similar in size to Samharam, is set on the western side of the Mesa on a small prominent platform. The building is around 50m long and 10m wide. The outer wall has collapsed. Within its footprint are some stone troughs. A slightly better-preserved walled building contains a substantial storage area, presumably for Frankincense

∽

### VISITING ANDHUR 17.570173, 54.709057

From the Clock Tower in central Salalah, the tarmac road to the mouth of the *wadi* 17.817519, 54.665173 is a 168km drive. Even the route taken by a rough track, below, eventually needs to travel through the *wadi* bed to reach the almost mythical Andhur. Wadi Andhur is a Nature Reserve, with signs noting access is by permit from www.meca.gov.om

Reaching Andhur is a chassis-buckling 40km drive directly through the boulder-covered bed of the eponymous *wadi*, as taken by Wendell Phillips, or a quicker but often impassable track from the Thumrayt to Marmul road at the turn into Fakhet at 17.796856, 54.561910. Be wary of this route's enticingly easy start. It winds through the hills west of the *wadi*, and even here, your chassis will still not easily forgive you. Discarded tyres by the roadside illustrate that, like the *wadi* route, it's a tyre shredding experience. There are several options to take from this main track towards the *wadi*. One option, has signage 'Wadi Anzur', indicating an approximate track, leading into the wadi. As track damage after heavy rain can often be localised, one route may be impassable, another possible to a capable driver and vehicle.

The author of this book has successfully driven on both the *wadi* and track routes and has also failed to negotiate both. Floods instantly make any track impractical, and the route may take months to become useable. The periodic cyclones that make landfall in Dhofar will cause damage to tracks that will take longer to become possible to drive along again. Indeed, at the best of times, a pair of Landcruiser or Nissan Patrol size 4x4 vehicles are required for safety, driven by very competent drivers.

This is a journey of difficulty, certainly not for a casual visit. As the actual archaeology is limited and the *wadi* here is not especially dramatic, this is far from a must-do. If venturing here, the vehicle's petrol tank should be as full as possible; engaging a 4x4 drive can use a surprising amount of fuel. Spare tyres should be checked before departure, and you should have ample drinking water in case the vehicle fails. Wearing comfortable walking shoes, a sun hat, and sunglasses will be ideal for exploring the location on foot. Naturally, though you will travel with more than one vehicle for safety, advise a responsible person of your plans and scheduled return time. Vehicle failure can be catastrophic, and pushing on, hoping the route becomes easier, may result in your driving into irretrievable locations.

# CHAPTER 8
# MUGHSAYL

# M UGHSAYL
المغسيل

Mughsayl Beach has thousands of visitors who pass close to a small historic settlement 'hidden' in full sight that is little visited.

*Mughsayl Beach*

WEST OF SALALAH IS THE EXTENSIVE BEACH OF Mughsayl. At the beach's western end, Wadi Ashawq winds for some 70km through Jabal Qamar, the mountains stretching west from Mughsayl towards Yemen. This *wadi*, with a catchment area of some 600 sq km, is the largest on the southern face of the entire Dhofar Mountain chain. The availability of underground water from the *wadi*, vast quantities of fish in the Arabian Sea and valuable Frankincense trees in the mountains around Mughsayl must have made this a desirable location for a settlement in historic times.

The geology of the Mughsayl area is chalky and fossil-rich: Limestone from the Oligocene period, 23-34 million years ago, through to the early Miocene, 20-23 million years ago. Gypsum is also found here; Oman is among the world's top 5 exporters of gypsum. Substantial geological faults running from west to east have been associated with the separation of the African and Arabian plates over the last 60 million years. At the beach's western end is rock overhanging horizontally above the sea. Short blowholes are found in the overhang, through which seawater can erupt as a fountain - this happens most reliably during the summer Monsoon. Behind the blowholes is Marnif Cave, a large open cave.

*Camels Mughsayl Beach*

The mouth of Wadi Ashawq is about 500 meters across as it enters the Arabian Sea. As with most *wadis* of Oman that exit into the sea, a Baymouth bar of sand closes its sea access. Reed beds of *Phragmites australis* and Mangrove, *Avicenia marina*, were found north of the road before the cyclone in 2018. In historical periods, before the road, when the Monsoon was more intense and created larger regular, but less intense, water flows, Wadi Ashawq's estuary was directly into the Arabian Sea. The temporary rebuild of the road from Salalah to the Yemen border away from the beach has resulted in a double lagoon. The small one upstream is of fresh water, and the one adjacent to the sea of brackish water. The replacement Salalah-Yemen road will be bridged across the *wadi*; this may alter the size of both lagoons.

In Mughsayl's surroundings, you can find Frankincense trees from just west of Salalah Port into Jabal Qamar & beyond into Yemen. The largest specimens are in the *wadis*, with smaller ones on the mountain slopes. On the mountain slopes, the endangered

Dragon tree, *Dracaena serrulate*, joins the Frankincense in adding some greenery to the otherwise barren landscape.

To the west of Mughsayl, Arabian Leopard *Panthera pardus nimr*, inhabit the arid mountains and escarpments. It is joined here by Arabian Wolf, *Canis lupus arabs*, Striped Hyaena, *Hyaena hyaena*, and Nubian Ibex, *Capra nubiana*, all of which are endangered in Oman and each species probably numbering less than 100 in Oman.

*Blowhole Mughsayl*

Birdlife is far more abundant; expect to see Arabian Partridge, *Alectoris melanocephala*, along the slopes of the *wadi*. The entire beachfront will have innumerable Gull (Siberian, *Larus heuglini*, & Sooty, *Ichthyaetus hemprichii*, etc.) and Tern (Caspian, *Hydroprogne caspia*, & Saunders, *Sternula saundersi*, etc.) and Osprey, *Pandion haliaetus*, at intervals along the beach.

*Frankincense trees Jabal Qamr*

JUST A SHORT WALK FROM THE WESTERN END OF Mughsayl beach, 230 meters northeast of the petrol station, is an ancient settlement, though many visitors to the beach overlook it. What is remarkable about this collection of buildings is that, given the bounty surrounding its location, the area of the entire settlement is remarkably small.

The buildings are on an elevated outcrop of rock a few meters above the bed of the *wadi*, just enough to raise them above flooding. The outcrop is about 170 meters long and has a maximum width of 40 meters on its western end.

In 1952-3, a team led by Wendell Phillips excavated the site. His team did not make a detailed archaeological report, calling the location a 'habitation' and assumed it was a fishermen's, settlement with what were noted as - water use areas, a mosque, and other rooms with uncertain functions. Juris Zarins was involved in limited survey/excavation in 1992-3 and again in 1995. He described incised red ware pottery (which seems to have been widespread in ancient Dhofar) at Mughsayl but little else concerning the site. In 2007, Brigham Young University excavated the location in pursuance of their association of this region with the journey (proposed to be a few decades after 600 BC) of the Mormon prophet Lehi with his son Nephi. They found a single pottery sherd, which they had dated to the 5th or 6th century BC.

The site has been fenced and later walled, since the 2012 excavation by the University of Pisa. If the site is opened for visits, the physical area occupied by buildings is at the western end of the outcrop. The area occupied by the buildings is not large at some 1,060sqmeters; the most significant room that creates part of the western wall, is believed to be the mosque and is less than 65sq meters. In the northwest of the building area is a water well, with associated rooms and drainage whose proximity to the mosque suggests an ablution area. Stone troughs add to the impression of an area for water use. There are fewer than 20 other small rooms of around 10 square meters each.

Settlement Mughsayl

Amongst the dated pottery found have been pre-Islamic 'dot & circle' jars (before AD 622) and shards of blue-glazed Abbasid period jars (in this case 750-950). A Dirham coin, also from the Abbasid period, has been found. Other finds include stone pipes for smoking, stone fishing net weights, and Scallop Shell oil lamp. The site has several periods of finds, suggesting occupation from the pre-Islamic through to around AD 1400.

Elsewhere in Wadi Ashawq, to the west of the raised outcrop, there are some smaller structures, including probable pre-Islamic graves.

Southwest of the archaeological site is Marnif Cave, which is immediately below a substantial olistolith rock (a mass of rock slump) near the sea. A path north of the rock leads up to a small archaeological site at the peak, which might be a watchtower or signal point for the principal archaeological site at Mughsayl. The view point comes after a steep climb on rock which, in places, can be slippy and therefore needs care.

## Visiting Mughsayl's archaeological site
## 16.883616, 53.776473

By itself, the site at Mughsayl would not demand a drive of 47km from Salalah. However, with the location near the much-visited beach and blowholes at Mughsayl, it is worth visiting – more so if driving on towards the west. If you have time to explore more, read from page 377 of my 5$^{th}$ Edition of the Oman guide for Bradt, which covers the journey to the Yemen border.

# CHAPTER 9
# AYN HAMRAN FORT

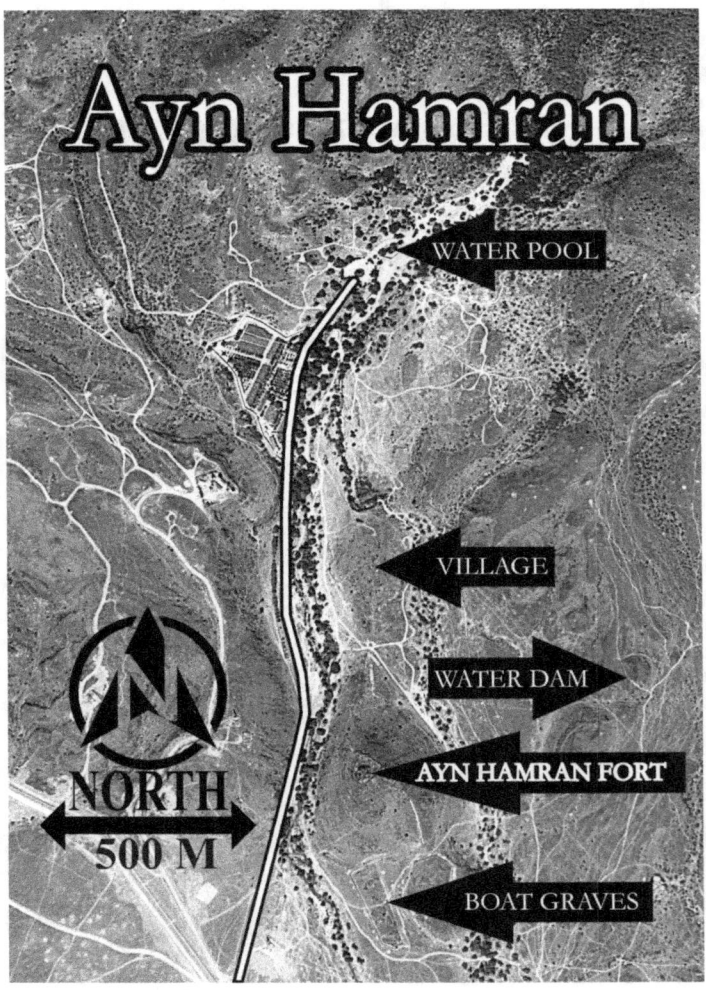

# Ayn Hamran Fort
قلعة عين حمران

One of Oman's best preserved ancient hilltop forts, Ayn Hamran Fort is, in origin, contemporary to its near neighbour Samharam.

## AYN HAMRAN FORT

NORTH OF THE SALALAH-MIRBAT ROAD, THE mountains leap up 600m above the plain. These mountains are Limestone from the Hadhramaut Group (56 million to 48 million years ago). Below the mountain's crest is the source for the permanent water spring Ayn Hamran. The water comes from a deep, narrow *wadi* that cuts into Jabal Qara, the central range of Dhofar's mountains.

The mountain's escarpment looks full of dead trees and bushes in springtime. However, the vegetation bursts into life from May in anticipation of the Monsoon. The scraggly small trees or large bushes seen are mainly *Anogeissus dhofarica*, which the steepness of the slope protects from livestock. But elsewhere in the mountains, they are under pressure because of overgrazing and cutting. Also found is *Maytenus dhofarensis*, which is endemic to Dhofar and whose spines make it popular to use in animal fences. A fruit and vegetable garden is west of the road towards the spring area.

The water here attracts a wide variety of wildlife, including birds. You may see various raptors riding the thermals, including Eagles such as Steppe Eagle *Aquila nipalensis*, Eastern Imperial Eagle *Aquila heliaca* and Verreaux's *Aquila verreauxii*. In bushes & trees, look for African Paradise Flycatcher *Terpsiphone viridis*, African Rock-Bunting *Emberiza cia* and on the slopes Tristram's Starling *Onychognathus tristramii*.

South of the spring, to the east of the road from the main highway, is a small conical hill about 30m high, with a hill fort, called Ayn Hamran Fort, on its summit. The location would have been defensible in a land without 'Torsion' or 'Trebuchet' type siege catapults, and it offers an excellent overview of the plain from the west through to the east. A modern fence encloses the fort; if the site is opened, the route up is via a steep flight of steps on the east side that takes you part of the way, with the rest of the ascent on a very loose surface.

The fort covers an area of around 7,100 sqm and comprises an internal keep surrounded by two walls. Most of the construction is made from Limestone with well-fitted drystone walls and limited use of mudbricks. Dr Juris Zarins partially excavated the fort in 1993-4, and he equates much of the construction and layout to the fortification of Ubar. Later surveys were done by the University of Pisa, which excavated Samharam.

*Steppe Eagle* Aquila nipalensis

Though the original entrance was on the western wall, today, a break in the eastern wall gives access, from the steps.

The external wall has 12 bastions, including three shared at the north with the inner wall. This external wall had several rooms in the northwest and probably a number along the eastern wall. The inner wall is remarkably similar to the original wall at Ubar. The inner wall's western, southern, and eastern sections have over 30 small cubicles opening onto the courtyard and three additional bastions. The central keep is now accessed via its southern wall from the courtyard. Divided into 9 chambers, the central keep is about 17x14 meters with well-built stairs leading up to a possible first floor or the roof.

The central keep was the first area of the fort to be built around 300 BC. Scattered in the area are several kiln-fired bricks; these may have been imported from Sohar in northern Oman. Substantial parts of the fort in Sohar are built from similar bricks, a highly unusual building material in Oman, though that current fort is later than Ayn Hamran. The use of Ayn Hamran Fort increased over the following centuries, and overall, it flourished on a similar time scale to Samharam.

*Ayn Hamran Fort*

The team found a small village on an adjacent low hill, approximately 370 meters north of the fort. The general area of this village has been badly disturbed; however, some excavations have suggested the remains of buildings constructed from undressed stones. There are two distinct phases of occupation, and the ruins excavated had part of a small ceramic Bull figure and many pottery shards.

Around 340 meters northeast of the fort, a small dam was located, which blocked a stream and had associated fields to its north and west. To the south of the fort are cemeteries enclosed within modern walling.

Stairs Ayn Hamran

The cemeteries western area have what are called 'boat-shaped' graves within it. In Dhofar, these boat-shaped graves overlap the pre-Islamic and Islamic periods. However, this cemetery has a scattering of microlith stone tools and 'grey ware' pottery, suggesting a pre-Islamic Iron Age date – broadly comparable to the fort.

∾

### VISITING AYN HAMRAN FORT 17.087244, 54.282395

Though not the most important archaeological site in Dhofar, Ayn Hamran Fort's general environment and ease of access, from the north of the Salalah-Mirbat road, after a 19km drive east from Salalah's Clock Tower, will make this worth visiting, on the way to or from Khawr Rawri, if the site is officially opened.

# CHAPTER 10
# QASBAR FORT

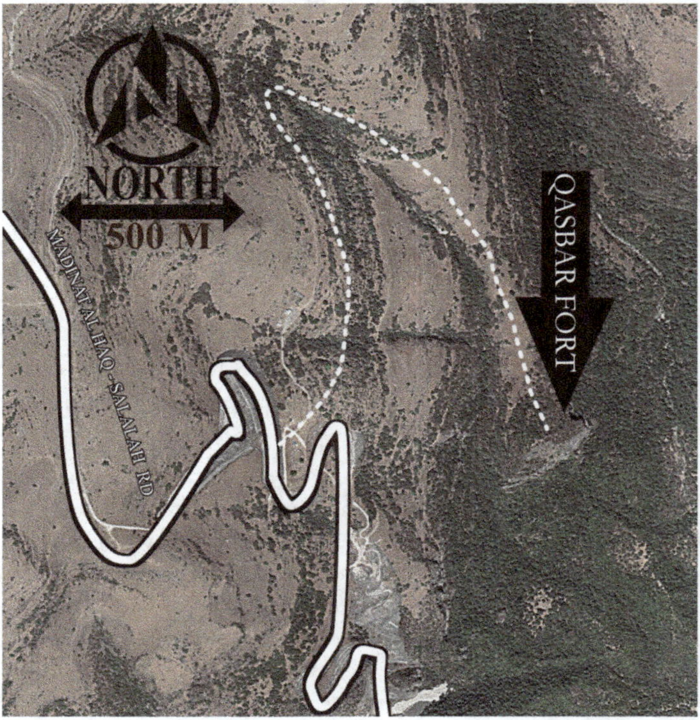

## Qasbar Fort
قلعه قصبار

Within the Dhofar Mountain's central, sea-facing, escarpment is Jabal Nashib, the area's most distinctive summit. Here is Qasbar Fort, a secure storage point for Frankincense.

∽

*Jabal Nashib*

QASBAR FORT (SOMETIMES GHASBAR FORT) OCCUPIES part of the summit of Jabal Nashib, one of the peaks in the crescent of mountains around Salalah. Jabal Nashib rises around 390m above the coastal plain. From the coast, less than 10kilometrs to the south, it appears as a pyramid within a broad valley. The choice of this peak may have given some extra security from attack due to the effort needed to reach it. A secondary or prime consideration may have been the panoramic observation it gave. The view has two practical aspects – to see people approaching the fort and perhaps ships drawing into Al Balid about 23kms to the southwest or Samharam, 15kms to the southeast. Ayn Hamran, is only 5kms to the southwest.

Despite its impressive shape when seen from the coast to the south, Jabal Nashib is less striking looking at it from the north, but still maintains that pyramid-like summit. From the north, the approach is initially down into a saddle (small basin) and up a broad ridge, more sharply, to Jabal Nashib's summit.

This area to Jabal Nashib's north accumulates soil, giving some fertile grazing below the main plateau to the north. In summer, the area has the usual scattered flowers of these mountains, their purple flowers contrasting with the new green leaf.

If you come where the vegetation is still in leaf, look for types of *Faboideae sp*, purple-flowered *Coleus barbatus* and stands of the pink-flowering *Impatiens balsamina*.

The dry *Impatiens balsamina* seed pods explode on touch – adding interest if walking after the monsoon season. *Becium dhofarense* is another flowing plant with pink/purple flowers. It grows in clusters of plants up to 2m high. The *Gladiolus sp (candidus/ ukambanensis)*, with trumpet-shaped white flowers, grows from corms. As usual in the escarpment area, the trees are dominated by *Anogeissus dhofarica*.

As the Monsoon approaches, the vegetation rapidly springs into life. The dampness encourages Arabian Cobra, *Naja arabica*, to explore, occasionally raising their head above the grass to see the source of any disturbance. This snake's colour varies, including almost brick red, honey, and dark brown. A walking stick is an ideal companion on this route. Its best taken in winter as the vegetation will have died back, and mist will not be cloaking the hills.

Impatiens balsamina

IN THE AREAS WHERE GRASS GROWS IN SUMMER, occasional regions of cleared vegetation show the activity of ants from the harvester Genus *Messor sp (foreli* etc*)*. Their trails show the latest source of seed.

Clearing made by Ants - below Qasbar Fort

Among the surprising animals that might wander through here, Arabian Leopard (*Panthera pardus nim)r* have been seen on the edge of roads leading up to the escarpment, Caracal (*Caracal caracal*) are also found in the general area, and Arabian Wolf, (*Canis lupus arabs)* are spread over the general plateau area.

Cattle - Jabal Nashib

Wandering over the landscape are innumerable cattle. They are released from their sheds on the upper plateau in the morning and will go home in the late afternoon. Before Dhofar's modern development, the local cattle were dwarf *Bos indus*. Since 1970, the introduction of European cattle (*Bos taurus* - Holstein-

Friesian & Jersey) has increased the size of many of these now hybrid animals. The cattle dung adds fertility to the ground.

About 200m west of Jabal Nashib is a small course for a seasonal stream. This creates part of the easiest route to get to Qasbar Fort – a circuitous U-shaped walk of around 2km from the suggested place to park a car. A faint path leads north from the parking and then, after crossing the stream's bare Limestone bed, the route makes the ascent north to Qasbar Fort. It crosses the saddle and is unclear but always towards Jabal Nashib. In the U bend of the walk are cave-like rock shelters, some having painted rock art.

No one has conducted excavations on Qasbar Fort yet, so there is little information available about it. Locally, it is ascribed to the Minjui, who ruled Mirbat's area from around AD 1087. They expanded from Mirbat (just over 40km southeast of Jabal Nashib) into Al Balid, ruling the region until around 1271 when Salim bin Idris al-Haboodhi, from Hadhramaut, defeated them.

Close to the summit of Jabal Nashib is the remains of a manmade ditch a couple of meters wide and a similar depth. Towards the summit, this ditch still has remnants of walling of natural rubble. The summit has steep natural slopes, with the south and east of Jabal Nashib having un-scalable cliff faces – and loose stones on the edges making them very easy to drop down. It must have had the best natural defences in the area.

Interior - Qasbar Fort

Close to the absolute summit are the remains of a building complex. The outline of a small chamber of about 3 sqm is near the summit. Apart from this chamber and the ditch is what was the purpose of the fortification. This is a windowless room of about 20m x 10m with a height of around 3 meters. Both the exterior and interior have lime plaster. This would have created a waterproof structure, assuming a good roof. Indeed, it's a far better construction than needed for livestock or everyday needs storage. This suggest storage of a valuable product, presumably Frankincense.

~

### VISITING QASBAR FORT 17.106426, 54.321094

Qasbar Fort is reached off the main Salalah – Mirbat Highway. Turn north on the roundabout, about 25 km east of the Clock Tower/Municipality in Salalah. Roads exit south to the Hawana Resort area and north to Ayn Tabraq, Ayn Athum. The tarmac road north eventually climbs up the escarpment past Qasbar Fort, and then around to Madinat Al Haq.

An unmarked exit just under 9km drive north of the roundabout has an open rough area 17.1040777, 54.3160767 (just east of the road) where it's possible to park before taking the walk above.

# CHAPTER II
# KHAWR RAWRI & SAMHARAM UNESCO SITE

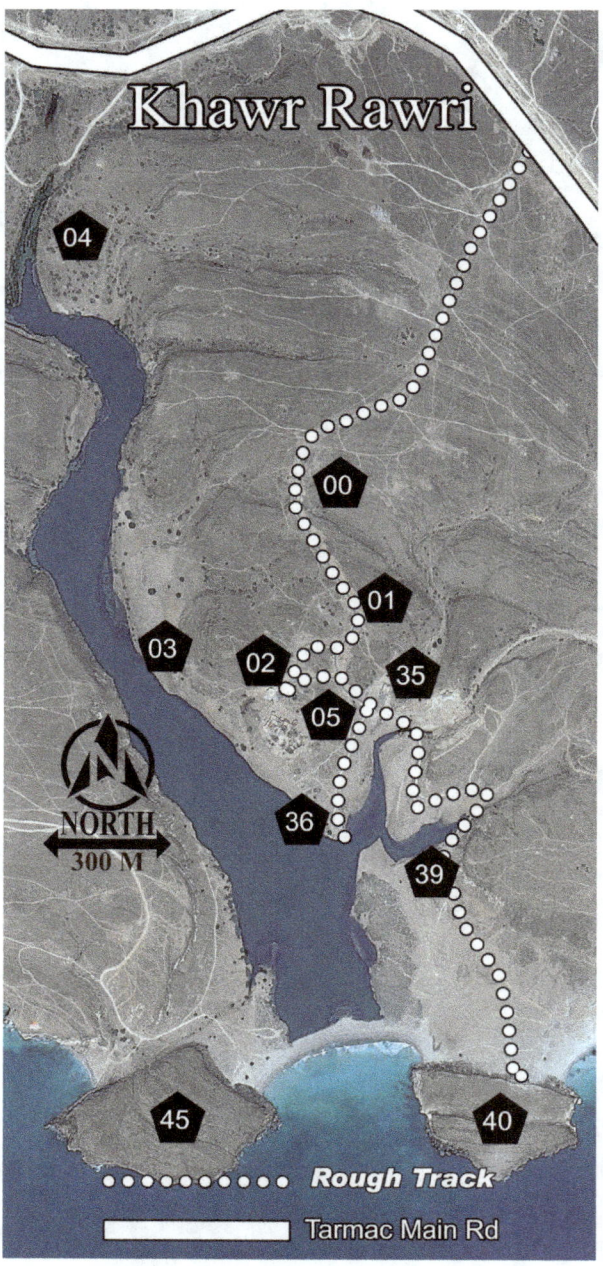

# Khawr Rawri & Samharam UNESCO Site
## خور روري و سمهرم

Legendary in all respects, the lagoon of Khawr Rawri shelters the ancient trading town of Samharam.

~

Almost forty kilometres east of Salalah, Khawr Rawri is a magnificent lagoon three kilometres long and up to 500 metres wide.

Making use of Khawr Rawri's sheltered location on one of the ancient world's developing trade routes was the ancient trading town of Samharam. The town traded with Africa, Europe, India, and beyond, for over 7 centuries before sinking into oblivion. At the southern end of the lagoon is the Baymouth sand bar, which currently separates it from the open waters of the Arabian Sea. For most of the trading history of Samharam, the Baymouth sand bar did not block the entrance, allowing even the largest boats of the period access to Samharam. Overlooking the entrance, and offering a landmark to the sailors who knew what lay behind them, are two prominent flat-topped mesas, one on either side of the lagoon's entrance. Each of these mesas has the remains of settlements, though these are far less obvious than Samharam.

Samharam is set about 20 meters above Khawr Rawri, on a low Limestone coastal plateau deposited 23-34 million years ago during the Oligocene period. To the north of Khawr Rawri is Jabal Al Qara – the central section of the Dhofar Mountains, which ascends sharply from the plain to over 600m above the level of the Arabian Sea. The plateau of Jabal Al Qara eventually rises to between 700-1000 meters high before dropping towards the north into Oman's Rub Al Khali Desert and central plain. These mountains are Karst Limestone from the Hadhramaut Group Umm Al Radhuma formation (56 million to 48 million years ago).

Khawr Rawri

While these mountains' steep southern sea-facing slopes have a seasonal cloud forest, the northern escarpment is an arid prelude to the desert a few kilometres away. Nestled within the sea-facing area is Wadi Darbat, the freshwater source for Khawr Rawri. Wadi Darbat and Khawr Rawri form an ecosystem running from the Jabal Qara plateau to the sea. Though not part of the World Heritage Site, Wadi Darbat plays an essential role in the ecology of the lagoon and its wildlife, and there are plans to incorporate Wadi Darbat and the entire Khawr Rawri area into a single Tourism administration area. During the summer Monsoon, the precipitation over Wadi Darbat's catchment area gives rise to the unexpected cloud forest of Dhofar along the sea-facing slopes. Springs currently feed most of the water in Wadi Darbat, and the increase in the water flow during the Monsoon refills perennial lakes along its length. The dominant trees on the mountain slopes are *Anogeissus dhofarica* and *Maytenus dhofarensis*, while close to the lakes are *Ziziphus spina-christi* (known in Oman as *Sidr* and elsewhere called Jujube) and Sycamore fig, *Ficus sycomorus*; with an especially large Tamarind, *Tamarindus indica*, towards the lake's northern end.

Mammals in the Wadi Darbat area include Arabian Leopard *Panthera pardus nimr*, Caracal *Caracal caracal schmitzi*, Genet *Viverra genetta* and Indian Crested Porcupine *Hystrix indica*.

An intense and persistent Monsoon may create enough water

flow that then cascades down from Wadi Darbat, occasionally as a waterfall, some 100meters over the natural Tufa dam at the southern end of Wadi Darbat. As Tufa is formed by precipitation of Lime from water, the age of this dam must be considerable. Occasional Cyclones, such as Mekunu and Luban on either side of the 2018 Monsoon, cause sufficient flooding to reopen a Baymouth bar that, in modern times, had entirely closed the lagoon.

Arabian Leopard (male)

Khawr Rawri is the largest natural inlet on the entire Dhofar coastline, and at its heart lies the ancient town of Samharam. Dr Alessandra Avanzini of the University of Pisa has been excavating the town of Samharam since 1996 and believes it is the most important pre-Islamic settlement in the Dhofar region. Samharam was, uniquely, given the name of the ruler during whose rule the town may have been founded in the third century BC. The Ancient Greeks referred to the site as Moscha Limen.

Theodore and Mabel Bent, who visited its ruined location in AD 1895, associated it with Abyssapolis, a town in the region also referred to by the Greeks. Samharam's history as a trading town covers over 700 years.

There is little vegetation in Khawr Rawri's immediate area except at the water's edge. Various Acacia species and occasional invasive *Prosopis juliflora* (Mesquite) are found. *Calotropis procera*, a milkweed called the silk plant, is scattered throughout the general area. Where this is the only obvious plant in an area, it is a sign of overgrazing, as it is poisonous, remaining while other plants are eaten.

*Professor Alessandra Avanzini at Samharam Excavations*

Khawr Rawri has an accumulation of gravel and silt along several sections of the lagoon's edge. This creates a habitat for rush, *Juncus rigidu*, bulrush, *Typha domingensis*, and sedge, *Cyperus conglomeratus*, providing cover for fish and various birds. These accumulated deposits are recent and date from flood events during the Holocene Epoch, 11,700 years ago to today. At the top of the bird-feeding chain in Khawr Rawri are the Black Kite, *Milvus migrans* and Osprey *Pandion haliaetus*. The Kites hunt over the central and southern edge of the

*Khawr*, while Osprey sit in Acacia trees on its southern edge, consuming the fish they have caught. Flamingos, *Phoenicopterus roseus*, Grey Heron, *Ardea cinerea*, Intermediate Egret, *Ardea intermedia*, Indian Pond Heron, *Ardeola grayii* and Squacco Heron, *Ardeola ralloides*, might be found in the water's edge; in the air, the Dhofar Swift, *Apus sp*, scream as they twist and turn in their hunt for insects. Smaller birds, such as the Pied Wheatear, *Oenanthe pleschanka*, and Tristram's Starling, *Onychognathus tristramii*, are often seen on the stones of Samharam while Arabian Partridge, *Alectoris melanocephala*, scuttle around at the northern end of Khawr Rawri. During winter, migratory birds might include White Stork *Ciconia ciconia*, Little Grebe *Tachybaptus ruficollis* and Ruff *Calidris pugnax*.

Samharam's elevated position on a slight rise some 20 meters above the lagoon at Khawr Rawri hints that some care was taken in selecting its location. It was both defensible and, with the southern edge of its hill lapped by Khawr Rawri's waters, allowed heavy loads to be manoeuvred down and onto waiting boats.

The firmest period for the foundation of Samharam is during the third century BC. However, carbon dated deposits from c1230 BC found under a room near the northerly gateway and main wall, is one of several carbon-dated finds that pre-date the probable foundation of the town. The location might have been the site for a small fishing village. Even the third century BC date precedes the Roman conquest of Egypt and Rome's subsequent entry into the Indian Ocean trade system.

The establishment of Samharam took place within the kingdom of Hadhramaut of southern Yemen whose capital, Shabwa, was at a hub on the Frankincense trade routes. A ruler of Hadhramaut was named Samharam, and it's his name that was used for the town. This is the only known example of the ruler's name being used for a southern Arabian settlement. The local word for the most important king in southern Arabia, before around the 1$^{st}$ century AD, was *Mukarrib*, and no two rulers would hold this title simultaneously. This King Samharam was one of the last *Mukarribs* of southern Arabia before the general political structures began to fragment.

Wadi Darbat - Waterfall

THE FIRST MENTION OF THE TOWN, WHICH SURVIVES IN Western literature, is in *The Periplus of the Erythraean Sea* 'Voyage around the Erythraean Sea'. This sea includes the Red Sea, the Arabian Sea and the Sea of Oman and is believed to have been written by a Greek merchant living in the first century AD Roman Empire who called Samharam 'Moscha' (also called Moscha Limen). His description reads -

Flamingo - Khawr Rawri

"Immediately beyond Syagrus the bay of Omana cuts deep into the coastline, the width of it being six hundred stadia; and beyond this there are mountains, high and rocky and steep, inhabited by cave-dwellers for five hundred stadia more; and beyond this is a port established for receiving the Sachalitic Frankincense; the harbour is called Moscha, and ships from Cana (near modern Bir Ali, Yemen) call there regularly; and ships returning from Limyrike and Barygaza (northwest and south west India respectively), if the season is late, winter there, and trade with the King's officers, exchanging their cloth and wheat and sesame oil for Frankincense, which lies in heaps all over the Sachalitic country, open and unguarded, as if the place were under the protection of the gods; for neither openly nor by stealth can it be loaded on board ship without the King's permission; if a single grain were loaded without this, the ship could not clear from the harbour." The Sachalitic country was also called the Land of Sakalan in some translations, the 'c' and 'k' are interchangeable. Despite ships being loaded from Samharam, no trace of a quay or jetty has been found. It may be that floods or cyclones have swept any remains away.

The conquest of Egypt by the Roman ruler Augustus in 30 BC, and the Roman absorption of the Nabataean kingdom in AD106 gave it command of the northern Red Sea. The flow of ships between Egyptian ports and India increased by 600% - many of which would call into Samharam for supplies or trade.

The Red Sea's southern area was also, eventually, under Roman control. Certainly, by AD110, Rome had stationed legions on the Farasan Islands in the far south of the Red Sea. The authorities there may have monitored the ship's cargo to assess it for a 25% Egyptian import tax or to ensure that the Egyptian export tax had been paid. Irrespective of the Legion's purpose on the islands, trade was dramatically increasing.

Though having its own network of trade links, Samharam was benefiting from the developing sea trading routes between the Roman world and the Indian subcontinent.

However, the collapse of the Hadramaut with its conquest by the Yemeni kingdom of Himyar (Himyarite) by the late 3rd century AD began a lengthy period of political instability in Southern Arabia. In addition, the religious changes brought about by the Roman establishment of Christianity as the state religion in AD 380 reduced Samharam's Frankincense trade over the subsequent period. A reduced monsoon also created a range of unfavourable issues. This caused a gradual silting up of Samharam's harbour and the eventual creation of a Baymouth sand bar that completely blocks the harbour entrance today. Trade evaporated as merchants looked elsewhere to earn an income.

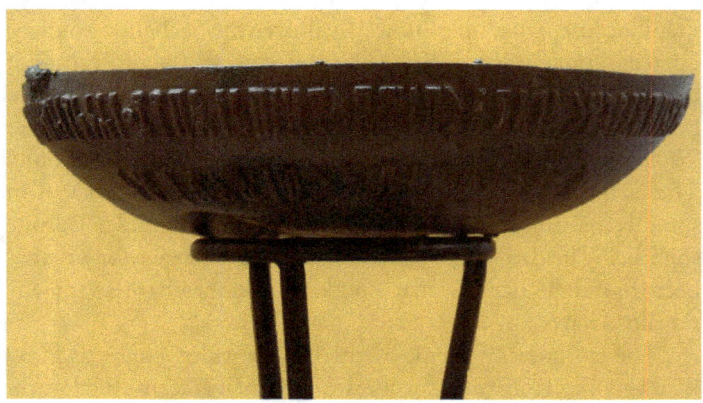

*Inscribed Bronze Basin - now on display in Al Balid*

In Samharam, Amphora from Kos, Greece, have been found.

A more general 'Dressel 2-4' style versions produced more broadly from around the Mediterranean, from around the end of the 1st century BC – 1st century AD have also been excavated. Other items include bronze Coins (often imitations of coinage from the Hadramaut), some as part of a coin hoard. A dated example of the King of Saba (Yemen) was from 80-100AD. Numerous glassware finds include glass beads and part of a Roman ribbed glass bowl in a cave outside the town to the north.

Bronze items include a Bell, Plaques, a Bronze Basin, and a Bronze Incense Burner. Bronze Candelabrum, a Horse shaped Bronze Rhyton (spout), Bracelet, Eastern Arabian imitation Coin of Alexander's tetradrachm.

*Bronze Rhyton - now on display Al Balid*

In AD 1895, Mabel and Theodore Bent, British explorers, published in the Geographical Journal the first modern reports about the ruins of Samharam to reach the west. Mabel wrote in her book 'Southern Arabia', "Surely there can be no doubt that this is the harbour which was anciently used by the merchants who came to this coast for Frankincense. It would be absolutely secure at all seasons of the year".

The initial archaeological investigations of the ruins took place in 1952 by Wendell Philips and his colleague Dr Albright. In the early 1960s, that team undertook their final excavations. Philips and his colleague Dr. Albright found some extraordinary artifacts, including a table with a bull motif and several objects inscribed with the name of the god Sin. Sin was the god of the Moon and wealth in pre-Islamic Hadhramaut. They removed various items, including inscriptions that noted the town's name, to the USA.

A team from Italy's University of Pisa, directed by Dr Alessandra Avanzini, started the current excavations in 1996 at

Samharam in conjunction with the Oman government. Their painstaking work has led to a greater understanding of the town's development and the discovery that it was established at least 100 years earlier than previously believed.

Today, many physical advantages that made Khawr Rawri such a superb location for a port in antiquity have changed. Reduced water flow from Wadi Darbat has allowed a semi-permanent 'Baymouth' sand bar to develop that blocks the exit into the sea (it was utterly destroyed during Cyclones Mekunu and Luban in 2018). Silt has also built up below Samharam, and this, together with land uplifting, has left the town some fifty metres away from the water's edge rather than immediately on it, as it must have been when founded.

With the great Tufa dam of Wadi Darbat overlooking Samharam and the two distinctive mesas on either side of Khawr Rawri's exit into the sea, this ancient site sits in a location that is as impressive today as it must have been to merchants arriving over two thousand years ago.

## KHAWR RAWRI AND SAMHARAM'S PHYSICAL SITES

**SITE00** The payment Kiosk, south of the Taqah – Mirbat Rd.

*Cave Tomb*

**SITE01** Around 650 meters after the payment kiosk, there are small cave tombs to the left (east) of the road. Created from a natural, shallow rock overhang, the main tomb is at the base of a short flight of six well-formed steps. This practice of burial within similar niches on the sides of *wadis* has been used in some places of Dhofar until recently. The excavating team believes the entrance may have been initially closed with large stones. Inside the tomb, a scattering of seashells, burnt bones, Roman glass, and a coin have been found, enabling its period to be dated. In antiquity, the tomb appears to have been looted, and more recently, it may have been used as a human shelter.

**SITE02** The information kiosk is at the parking and entrance into the walled town. Toilets are here - in addition to those behind the small museum. A path leading northwest from behind the information kiosk at Samharam takes you along the lagoon's edge some 250m from the town to SITE03.

**SITE03** the University of Pisa, named this building the 'temple *extra muros*' (Temple outside the walls). It was constructed during the same era as the earliest phase of Samharam.

The principal room is almost square in ground plan, just under seven meters on each side, with an L-shaped external antechamber. The interior has the remains of two bench-like platforms that may have provided a base for two pillars on each. Between these is a column, identified as an altar. Several incense burners, including some made from seashells and one made from stone with three rows of 'dentils' have been discovered here by archaeologists.

*Temple* extra muros'

A coin of Amdan Bayin, King of Saba, who ruled from about AD 80-100, helped with dating when it was found. The late first century AD probably saw the abandonment of the temple, possibly due to a flood. After that event, the area was frequently flooded from Wadi Darbat. As with the cave tomb, there is evidence of more recent use as a temporary dwelling.

**SITE04** Upstream from Samharam, towards Wadi Darbat, is an extensive cemetery on the east bank, with numerous oval 'Boat-Shaped' Graves. The walk to reach these is along rough, rocky surfaces of almost two km one way from the carpark at Samharam or about 1.5 km from the temple Extra Muros. The graves are about 400 meters south of the old Taqah-Mirbat road as it crosses the *wadi*. These Boat-Shaped Graves, each with massive upright stones, are common throughout the coastal Dhofar region and have generally been dated to before the period of Islam through to c AD 900; the date given for these specific graves is around AD 880, making them Islamic. The *wadi* continues upstream (north under the road bridges) to the Tufa dam at Wadi Darbat.

*Boat-Shaped Graves & the Tufa Dam of Wadi Darbat*

ROUGHLY RECTANGULAR, SAMHARAM IS approximately 130 metres wide (northwest-southeast) and, from the northerly gate (hereafter 'Town Gate' – the principal fortified entrance) to the rear wall, some 67 metres. The town's area is comparable to a smaller medieval castle in Europe, for example, Caernarfon Castle or the main keep of Spis Castle. Dr Avanzini and her team from the University of Pisa calculated that it covers 8,500 square meters, with 7,000 square meters available within its thick town walls. This area may have been home to between 2-

300 people living in approximately 30 buildings. Even compared to other ancient southern Arabian towns, Samharam does not cover a large area.

Despite centuries of occupation and many internal changes, the town's external walls have remained fixed in their location since they were built. The town's population must have remained steady over the years because it was a trading outpost rather than growing as an organic centre of the local population. Functionaries of the state, security and religion must have been a substantial part of the population. Dr Alessandra Avanzini says it is, by far, the most substantial fortification known from historic Dhofar. The value of the trade in Frankincense enabled Shabwa, over 800kms away, to maintain this isolated but impressive town.

Samharam's first significant building was the 'Monumental Building 2' (the 'Monumental Building 1' retains its name as it was excavated before this). It is of a comparable date to the Town Gate. The Monumental Building 2 was built in what could be called Phase 1 before the town's walls were built. After initial trading success, the first stages of the Town Gate were constructed during Phase 2 along with much of the northern wall that extends on either side of the gate. The northern wall was extended during Phase 3, including the two towers to its east and west. The entire western wall was completed during Phase 3, as was a short section leading south from the northeast Tower. During Phase 4, the southern wall and final section of the eastern wall were finished. Phase 4 also saw the creation of the 'Monumental Building 1' and its water well. The northwestern temple and small cultic temple, south of the 'Monumental Building 1', were built during Phase 5, and the Town Gate area was enlarged. During Phase 6, the walls of 'Monumental Building 1' were substantially thickened; work on the Town Gate and two free-standing towers near the northern wall was also undertaken. During Phase 7, the massive barrier wall at the Town Gate's entrance was erected along with external structures to the northeast Tower and a free-standing tower close to the eastern wall. Many internal buildings were built, altered, and rebuilt during these Phases. The changes were greatest in the area south of the Town Gate.

These Phase numbers and subsequent building numbers are the author's choice to ease understanding and facilitate cross-referencing between text and map. The University of Pisa's academic enumeration was given in order of the date a site was excavated.

The town has a path around the exterior. However, for the visit suggested here, the entry and exit are made through the impressive Town Gate, which is easy to see from the car park, and the route within the town is taken in an anticlockwise direction (right turn after passing through the gate).

**SITE 05** The Town Gate was massively re-fortified several times, protecting the northern approach to the town, which was more vulnerable to attack. The other sides of the town are protected by natural steep slopes up to the walls and, to the southwest, the lagoon's water.

The stonework within the Town Gate's passage had several dedicatory inscriptions carved into it. Two inscriptions now remain, the most interesting of which describes the construction of Samharam.

*Camel and Town Gate*

"Sdm Tlm, son of Qwmn, the servant of Ilidhdh Yalut, who was the king of Hadhramaut, was an inhabitant of the city of Shabwa and directed the construction works. Its blocks of roughhewn and polished stone, its realisation from its base to its top and the construction and structures of its components were at the behest and order of his lord Abiyatha Salan, the son of the Dhamarali chief of the Hadrami military detachment of the Sakalan land".

When the Town Gate area was first constructed, the entrance was through an L-shaped gated passage, which lay within the town except for two external bastions. Holes for 'drawbar' gate closures can be seen in the stonework. A postern gate, SITE34, was set within the eastern bastion. Successive additions to the main gated passage increased its length beyond the walls and changed its shape to a zigzag. Zigzag entrances are common in Southern Arabia; certainly, while they would reduce the impact of any direct assault, it is also thought that ancient people believed Jinn (genie) would be prevented from entering by the shape.

The final addition to this Town Gate area was a substantial stone barrier to prevent overwhelming frontal attacks, perhaps by battering ram, against the doors. Today, visitors enter the Town Gate through those more recent additions and step into the town through the gate's original section.

**SITE06** Entering the town from the Town Gate's passage, a five-roomed building is immediately in front. Like many other buildings within Samharam, animal bones, seashells, pottery pieces and charcoal were found within the floor area material. Though there were stairs inside the building, the structure may not have had a second story; possibly it was simply a flat-roofed single-story building.

*Inscription in Town Gate*

**SITE07** Behind building SITE06 is one of the town's essential constructions, the 'Monumental Building 1' that dates from Phase 4. Wendell Phillips and his excavation team identified it as a temple; later, researchers believed it was a palace. Today it is assumed that it had a more prosaic function, as a massive defensive structure for the town's most essential resource, water. The entrance is just south of building SITE06, and, as with the Town Gate, this was originally a zigzag entrance. Inside this Monumental Building 1, to the right from the entrance, is a staircase about 180cm wide; it must have allowed access for several people at the same time. The well has a depth of some 25 metres and is lined with extremely well-formed, smooth stone slabs. These slabs are probably structurally unnecessary as the shaft was cut through solid rock.

However, the slabs also created a higher top for the well; this might have been a deliberate design to prevent liquids from flowing into the well. There are clear signs of rope friction on the blocks within the well. From a stone basin, a channel could conduct liquid from this building to the town's exterior through stone trough-like channels. The width of the northern wall of Samharam, which is shared by the Monumental Building 1, was increased (from the exterior of the town) after it was first built, perhaps to support the original wall. This wall is the thickest in the entire town, between 9 and 10 meters wide.

The Town Gate and northern wall leads to speculation why such substantial defences were needed. Local peoples both supplied and were beneficiaries of Samharam's trade, for them to attack the town would provide little benefit; unless they were compelled to make the supply of Frankincense. The major regional power in opposition to Hadramaut was the Kingdom of Himyar. The periodic improvements in defence suggest that whoever caused the need was a constant, long term threat.

**SITE08** From Monumental Building 1, turning right into the town leads to an area whose function has changed over time, from being a public area to finally having small buildings. The excavated building had a plastered floor and, in its southwest, a small staircase supported by a pedestal. Artefacts found in the layers that covered this area included bronze coins, a ring, and an iron javelin head. The building may have been

*Monumental Building 1*

two storeys high and had open fireplaces on the ground floor, possibly furnaces. Below the building charcoal was found and carbon dated to at least 470 BC. The quantity of metals, coin blanks and metal slag found in Samharam suggests that metalworking occurred within the town. People may have traded the metal from other regions of Arabia and India in exchange for Frankincense resin.

**SITE09** Immediately south of the Monumental Building 1 is a small complex of three rooms, two of which abut directly onto the wall of Monumental Building 1. Stone equipment, including stone tools, hand-mills, pestles, polishers, and whetstones, was found within the floor layers. Other finds include a whale vertebra and numerous coins; perhaps this was a butchery. At a later period, the rooms were completely reconfigured.

**SITE10** Immediately south of SITE09, this building is a very late phase enlargement of SITE09. These rooms were built during the time that two of the rooms of SITE09 were restructured. These new rooms may have been extra living space, as the original building was being used commercially.

**SITE 11** Just west of building SITE 10, is a building that is separate from other buildings that have been excavated so far. The east entrance leads into an oblong hall, from which rooms on either side could be accessed. The rooms underwent alteration during the building's life; for instance, the entrance hall was originally a single room and a dividing wall was built, creating two rooms. The building's finds include a pendent seal with four Ancient South Arabian letters and a stele with a crude incised face.

*Cultic Shrine under excavation*

**SITE12** North of building SITE11 is identified as a 'Cultic Shrine' from Phase 5, though it was subsequently altered several times. This shrine was built on top of earlier buildings and was entered from the west. An altar area with Limestone columns decorated with vipers formed the south wall (these are now removed to a museum). The location also yielded limestone incense burners during the excavation. Look for a bronze Lion about 10 cm long in the Archaeological Gallery (see SITE 35 below); this Lion was excavated from within the floor area of this shrine. The largest object found here has been an 'offering table' measuring 87cm long.

**SITE 13** Against the northern wall of Samharam is a small building. This is the most westerly building along the town's northern wall. Its two rooms are just under 6m long and relatively narrow. Stairs in one room led to a second floor. Part of an Ivory tusk and an Egyptian amphora have been excavated within the building. An empty 'Boat-shaped' grave about 110cm long was found in the southeast corner of the building. Its construction made clear that the two walls that formed the corner were intact when the grave was created.

*Northwest area of Samharam*

**SITE 14** To the northwest of Samharam is a tower. This Tower, an early phase construction, was entirely rebuilt and enlarged during the historical occupation of Samharam. The rebuild appears to have been done around the same time that work on increasing the size of the town wall at Monumental Building 1 was undertaken. In the Tower's area, debris excavations revealed carved stonework, lime plaster decoration of Ibex, and a bronze lamp.

*Temple to the God Sin - the stone trough is now in Oman Across Ages museum.*

**SITE 15** A complex of rooms on the northern part of Samharam's western wall has been identified as a Religious Temple.

This is dedicated to the god 'Sin', perhaps the same as the Mesopotamian god Sin of the Moon and Wealth, millennia earlier. The Religious Temple was constructed on top of an earlier building, and over the lifespan of the town, the temple area was enlarged. The entrance is up a small flight of stairs into an L-shaped courtyard. A large stone trough, looking as if it was abandoned, was removed from here to the Oman Across Ages museum. A flight of stairs would have led to a second story. To the right of these stairs is a room interpreted as the main sanctuary. This room may have had eight columns to support the upper story. Votive objects found scattered on the floor of the temple included a bronze bowl with a dedication to the god Sin, in "his temple in Samharam in the land of Sakalan', (this can be seen at the Museum in Al Balid), bronze incense burners and a votive plate with a human figure. A stylised horse figurine that formed the spout of a bronze Rhyton (a tubular drinking spout) found here is now also displayed in the Al Balid Museum. The temple's dedicatory inscriptions are believed to have been on bronze plaques, hung on the walls – and presumably removed at some time. A Limestone Incense Burner excavated in the temple has a crescent moon decoration with a palm tree and Ibex. As with many other areas in the town, several Scallop shells and *Chlamys townsendi*, used for incense burning, were found. The more attractive Abalone shell, *Haliotis mariae*, found east of Mirbat, is absent from Samharam. It may be that Mirbat and the area to its east were beyond the control of the ruler of Samharam.

**SITE 16** Southeast of the Religious Temple SITE 15 and immediately north of the substantial walls of the Monumental Building 2 SITE 17 is a small building. This is 11m long and 5m wide with two rooms and access areas for its stairs. It appears to have been built on a previously unbuilt area and, in its northern part, on an 'accumulation of cultural deposits'. Probably built at the same time as the construction of this building was the staircase to the south, lying against the Monumental Building 2. The stairs must have been used to access higher parts of the Monumental Building 2. Much of building SITE 16 had considerable disturbance and remodelling over the years and evolved from a primarily residential building into one where plaster or mortar made from Limestone was produced.

**SITE 17** South of the Religious Temple, SITE 15 is a substantial building called 'Monumental Building 2'. This was the first major structure of what became Samharam. There is no hint of any previous building activity as they constructed the building directly onto the bedrock. The exterior walls are massive, up to 2.5m thick and may have been 7m in height, judging from the volume of debris. Mud bricks have been used within the structure and the stone surfaces had a plaster finish. The structure comprised three rooms, the largest with six columns supporting a platform above. No trace of an entrance at ground level has been excavated; perhaps the stairs associated with SITE 16 gave access to an entrance on the upper floor.

Oil lamps, an incense burner, and Egyptian amphora were found within the 'Monumental Building 2' building. Pottery from Aksum (Ethiopia & Eritrea) and from southern Arabia was found. The characteristic 'Rouletted Ware' pottery from the ancient southern Indian port of Arikamedu in Tamil Nadu was also excavated and dates to the early second century BC and later first century AD. Local pottery in Samharam was slab-made rather than wheel-thrown and used the same material as the town's mud brick walls. This method is much the same as pottery made in the region today, for example, the cuboid-shaped incense burners. Images of Camels have been found carved directly onto the stone of the walls, along with Ibex, an animal frequently portrayed in southern Arabia in semi-religious contexts.

**SITE 18** Just west of the Monumental Building 2 is a small irregular street or court, where a Pottery Kiln was excavated. The diameter of the Kiln is around 140cm, with an additional area for men to work this would have taken up much of the space in the street. This use of street space emphasises how inelastic the area of the town was. They partially sunk the Kiln in a pit for the fire and it was partially built above ground for the pots. The upper section may have been destroyed and rebuilt after each firing. Iron, Bronze, Bitumen, and vitrified Pottery are among the range of materials associated with this Kiln.

From this Pottery Kiln area, a walk over towards the southeast of the town leads past an access point to a **Viewing Area** over the lagoon of Khawr Rawri. On the opposite bank can be seen the rapidly expanding suburb of Taqah. The two promontories of the Inqitat Taqah SITE 44 (west) and Inqitat Mirbat SITE 39 (east) sit on either side of the location of a Baymouth bar (a sandbar barrier). This Baymouth bar could not have existed 2,000 years ago due to far greater rain and water flow down from Wadi Darbat. This Viewing Area is an excellent point to scan the lagoon for any interesting birds around the water, especially with Binoculars, as the view to the Baymouth bar is just under a kilometre away.

**SITE 19** To the southeast of Samharam, after the viewing area and just south of a small Acacia tree, is a building thought to have been a reconstruction of an earlier building. Two rooms, one almost square and the other oblong, have been excavated. A scattering of 2.5kg iron slag, beads, and pendants have been discovered in one room, along with a furnace; here, the excavations by Wendell Phillips are believed to have found 'coin blanks'. Stone tools found here include polishers, pestles, mortars, and whetstones. Several vertebrae of Whales have been found in the building, and these are thought to have been used as stools. This was probably a workshop.

**SITE 20** A little northeast of building site19, on this route, is a building with two long rooms, a small annexe at the southwest of about 1.5x1.5 meters and three adjacent rooms to the north. The annexe had a range of objects excavated from it, including iron slag, lead, a bronze bracelet, and a crucible fragment. Stone stairs ascend to an upper floor in the central long room. Ash from animal bones was discovered in open fireplaces found at both ends of the central long room.

In the southeast corner of the town, diagonally opposite the temple, is the raison d'être of the town, its Frankincense resin storerooms. Although the Greek chronicler of *The Periplus of the Erythraean Sea* wrote that heaps of Frankincense resin were lying around unguarded, these storerooms suggest that Frankincense resin was, in fact, carefully protected. This storage complex's initial construction is from the town's early years. Coins and a second-century Egyptian alabaster piece have been found here.

**SITE 21** On the right is a room with a central platform for the bases for five pillars. This room was a later addition to the Frankincense resin storage area. It's to the west of the principal access hall for these rooms. They lime-plastered the floor of the room and applied gypsum coating to the walls. This not only prevented any precious Frankincense resin from falling between the stones but also weatherproofed the room to ensure that the Frankincense was stored in good condition.

**SITE 22** This room, which would have provided secure access to most of the Frankincense storerooms, has a single entrance to the west and a gateway at SITE 24 at the east from which a route from Samharam goes down to the water of Khawr Rawri. Both doorways had a ramped floor to allow easier access in and out of the room. Only a few objects have been recorded here, with scattered pieces of a bronze bowl with inscriptions (in the style of the bronze bowl from the temple SITE 15) and the iron blade of a weapon. This room may have functioned as a trading room between the town's merchants, its ruler, and the visiting ships. It may have represented a secure area to make ready Frankincense for dispatch. Towards the town's final period, the western door, which gave access into this room, was blocked, the floor was raised, and the only access was from the eastern gate SITE 24.

*Southeast of Samharam*

**SITE 23** To the south of room SITE 22 is a complex of six storage rooms - SITE 23. The interior of these rooms was covered with a heavy cement-like plaster. The University of Pisa believes they were for storing Frankincense resin. However, other valuable products could equally have found space here. Wendell Phillips's team previously excavated these rooms. The access to these rooms was either high in the walls or from the roof, as no ground based doorway has been excavated. This is similar to granaries within administrative areas in Lower Nubia in Egypt's Middle Kingdom. Access there also being from either the roof, or high in the wall. The room, SITE 23a, just to the south of the exit SITE 24, had a door giving access into room SITE 21 and a second door into the room SITE 23b, immediately to its south. It's easy to imagine that these two rooms were an office and sleeping place for the supervisor of the storehouses. At a late date, both doors were blocked; perhaps at the time, the western door in room SITE 22 was also sealed.

*Eastern gate to Samharam*

**SITE 24** The eastern gate from the town, SITE 24, was restored in 2012. Excavating debris from around walls in archaeological sites reduces the wall's support and increases the risk of their collapse. Heavy rains in 2007 and 2012 accelerated the likelihood of collapse in many parts of Samharam. All stones around this exit were, therefore, enumerated and visually recorded. This allowed the area to be consolidated so the stones could be removed and returned more stably to their original location. Outside this gate is the perimeter path around the town. It gives excellent views of the lagoon and towards a wooden Dhow SITE 37, which is written about below.

**SITE 25** north of room SITE 22 are more storage rooms, and once again seem to have been accessed from high in the wall or roof. **SITE 26** north of the exit SITE 24 is a tower, which is free-standing outside the town and accessed from the perimeter path. The Tower is roughly 16sqmeters and was almost entirely covered by the archaeological mound of debris. The town's general walling is drystone, with thicker walls being double-walled with stone debris and sand infill. The stone used is local; for example, a small Limestone quarry is west of Taqah. Mud brickwork was used in some areas, and the University of Pisa team believes this was the case for the upper floors of buildings. The mudbrick's collapse and the failure of the stone walls created the debris that almost wholly obscured Samharam. This then became a 'Tell', the archaeological mini-hill of the Middle East. The word Tell comes from the Arabic meaning hill.

The exterior of SITE 24 tower's north wall was destroyed, and this damage had spread to the northern ends of both the western and eastern walls, though the southern wall of the Tower was in good condition. It has, therefore, been consolidated and rebuilt.

As with other restored areas in the town, the rebuilt levels of the Tower and walls can be identified by a 'geotextile' layer, which shows the junction between untouched stonework below and the rebuilt level above; the geotextile layer also adds some protection to the original layer below it. A mix of sand, crushed stone, and 95% lime was used for the mortar, and a rubble infill was used for the core.

*Eastern area of Samharam*

**SITES 27/28/29** The northeastern corner of the town is marked by bastion-type towers. In contrast to the smaller stones used in Samharam's interior, the builders utilized massive Limestone blocks, often more than 100 cm wide, for the construction of most of the exterior walls of the bastion-type towers. Tower SITE 27 was built after tower SITE 29, on which it leans, and before the tower SITE 28 which also leans on SITE 29. The core of TOWER SITE 28 is made of two chambers, possibly to reduce the structure's overall weight and outward pressure on its external walls; they may also have allowed men warding off the attack to be protected inside.

**SITE 30** west along the northern wall is another free-standing tower located outside the town and accessed from the perimeter path. Ancient debris and excavated waste from the Phillips excavations obscured this Tower. Careful examination of the debris, by the University of Pisa revealed bronze objects, an arrow fragment, a finger ring and four bronze coins. The renovation was made as with the tower SITE 26.

**SITE 31** With four rooms, this building, southeast of the Town Gate, may originally have been excavated by the expedition of Wendell Phillips. Inside, a room was re-excavated by the University of Pisa in 2008. This room, located in the southwest of the building, appears to have had flooring made with reused limestone slabs. A large stairwell occupied much of this room, and three stairs are still in place. The original entrance to this room was via the building's southern wall. Later, this entrance was blocked, and a new one was made on the western wall of the building.

**SITE 32** Against the northern wall and immediately east of the Town Gate is one of Samharam's first buildings. It was probably created at the same time as the northern wall of the town. Initially, it had four rooms, and after a short period, during which it appears to have been abandoned, the floor was rebuilt, and stairs were added to the building's rear. A final building phase circa AD 300 created an additional entrance room on the building's southern wall. This reduced the public street area, but now this entrance is hardly noticeable above the surface. Charcoal pieces excavated below the building's strata have been carbon-dated to at least 900 BC, with one piece to 1230 BC. These ancient signs of human activity indicate what a favoured location Samharam is in.

**SITE 33** south of building SITE 32 is a building that was partially excavated in the 1950s. This building has its entrance opening into the principal street running south from the Town Gate complex. Located in a prime location, it must have been the largest house in Samharam. The building had several rooms on the ground floor and finds here include a pit filled with bones and shells along with remains of fires within the floor of the room, on the right before the entrance steps. Inside and opposite the entrance to the house, at the end of a hall, are stairs. Amongst the finds here have been a glazed jug, soft-stone vessels, and metal slag. The building was reconfigured extensively during its use, with new flooring overlying the original, and its walling was rebuilt and repositioned.

**SITE 34** Exiting Samharam through the Town Gate SITE 05 there is a small Postern Gate SITE 34 on the right. This appears to have been part of the original gateway's construction. This postern gate was excavated and stabilised in 2012 to re-enable its use today. It is a narrow Z-shaped passage and offers an alternative route out of Samharam.

While the town of Samharam is the principal structure in Khawr Rawri, there are several other sites, which add interest to a visit.

**SITE 35** To the northeast of Samharam is a modern building, the Archaeological Gallery, with a limited number of items on display and exhibits about Samharam and its region. Look for the room that has a 'looped' video about Oman. There are toilets to the rear and, to its east, an isolated Modern Theatre SITE 36.

**SITE 37** Immediately to the right (east) of the Archaeological Gallery, the foundations of several ancient houses, each with a square, well-defined outline, were found. These date to the same period as Samharam, as illustrated by an excavated coin of Yashhuril Yuharish, son of Abiyasa, King of Hadhramaut. He is believed to have ruled in the late first century BC – early first century AD). It is possible that these satellite buildings associated with Samharam had a connection to agricultural or herding activity in the area.

Sambuq Al Dhib - with named inscription

**SITE 38** Here is part of an original *Sambuq*-type Dhow called

*Al Dhib* (The Wolf). This was constructed in 1953 and was based in Sadh, 70km east of Samharam, as the Eagle flies. The word *'Sambuq'* for a particular type of ship is quite old; Ibn Battuta wrote that he sailed on several of these within the north Arabian Sea on his voyages between AD 1325 and 1347. The word 'Dhow' seems to have been used for an Arab warship as recorded in the 18$^{th}$ century by the English East India Company, and the name stuck and became a generic for any Arab ship. *Sambuqs* were the most common Arab sailing ship. The replica of *Al Dhib*, next to it, was constructed in 2012.

The rough track that skirts the east of the lagoon for about 1,600meters from the Archaeological Gallery leads to the eastern of the two promontories that are such a distinctive feature of Khawr Rawri (do not venture into the private land beyond the modern fence even if the gates are open).

**SITE 39** On the track at about 840meters from the Archaeological Gallery on the very edge of the lagoon are the remains of a small building, of about 8meters x 10meters. This building is a mosque, with a Mihrab on the western wall and steps down to the lagoon. The rooms previously had columns and a lime-plastered floor. They later reused part of the building materials to construct a slightly smaller structure with a small antechamber on top of the original. It may date to AD 800-900.

**SITES 40/41/42/43/44** The two promontories have scattered archaeological remains. Inqitat Mirbat **SITE 40** (the eastern one, also called Al Hamr Al Sharqiyyah), where the track leads, is fortunately the more interesting. It does, however, require a steep walk up (and afterwards down) along a simple rough path of stone and sand. This location may interest a limited number of visitors as the remains are less extensive than at Samharam. The promontory has a northern wall of just over 650meters, which may have had occasional towers that might defend a settlement. About 2/3rds of the way along the wall is a gated complex with two towers, **SITE 41**, dated to the Islamic period, before the 12$^{th}$ century AD. The northeast area was a small settlement, **SITE 42**, extending about 140meters along the main defensive wall. A scattering of imported glazed pottery from the base of the wall suggests a trading centre was enclosed by it.

Much of the walling was found below the current ground level due to the collapse of the structures, along with windblown sand and soil filling it in. The eastern end of Inqitat Mirbat has several circular structures, **SITE43**, which may date to the Bronze Age. The western end (overlooking the Baymouth bar) is an Islamic complex SITE44, which dates to the period after Samharam was abandoned. Scattered over the mesa are shell middens of around 10m diameter and up to 2m thick. These are contemporary with Samharam and dated to around 270 BC.

*Inqitat Mirbat*

**SITE45** It is usually possible to walk across the Baymouth bar to Inqitat Taqah **SITE45**, which has some archaeology comparable in date to Inqitat Mirbat.

Baymouth Bar - Khawr Rawri

### Visiting the UNESCO World Heritage Site of Khawr Rawri and Samharam 17.036463, 54.436194

Khawr Rawri and Samharam is an extensive site with well-excavated ruins and interesting associated features. Any visit will be made in full sun on generally unpaved paths, so appropriate clothing and carrying some water is suggested. Though outside Salalah, just off the main Salalah-Mirbat Road, this is an easy drive of 30 minutes east from central Salalah. Any visit will take over an hour or longer if you are interested. The entrance charge for a non-resident of Oman is OMR3 (child OMR1).

*Incense Burner excavated at Samharam - with image of Lion and Ibex - now in Oman Across Ages museum*

# CHAPTER 12
# AL BALID UNESCO SITE

130  LAND OF FRANKINCENSE

# Al Balid UNESCO Site
البليد

The medieval town called Dhofar (often historically Zafar), now named Al Balid, was a wealthy port in modern Oman's southern Governorate of Dhofar. Known in medieval times to people from Morocco to China, Al Balid built its fame as an entrepot for trade in an extraordinary range of goods, including Frankincense resin, Horses, and Silk.

∽

THE SURROUNDS OF THE MEDIEVAL TOWN OF AL BALID have changed little since it was visited by Ibn Battuta and Zheng He in its heyday 700 years ago.

The town is situated on a coastal plain at the base of the central crescent shaped section of the Dhofar Mountains named Jabal Qara. These ascend sharply over 600meters above the level of the coastal plain. Jabal Qara's plateau eventually rises to between 700-1000meters high before dropping towards the north into Oman's Rub Al Khali Desert and central Oman plain. Jabal Qara is principally Karst Limestone from the Hadhramaut Group Umm Al Radhuma Formation (56 million to 48 million years ago). The coastal plain is conglomerates, silt, and clays.

Rising summer temperatures over distant northern India and Arabia's interior draws winds onto the coast from the southwest Arabian Sea from May to September. This increase in heat, to some 50c, is the engine of the Indian Ocean Monsoon. The wind streams from the southwest past Tanzania, Kenya, and Somalia in Africa, then crosses the sea to the coast of Oman near Al Balid. The continual winds drag surface water towards the northern end of the Arabian Sea, which lifts cool water from the ocean depths. It is this cold-water mass that eventually collides with Oman's southern coast.

Jabal Qara forms a barrier blocking the wind of the summer Indian Ocean Monsoon; the mountains crescent shape also helps concentrate the monsoon's effect. The chilly sea water helps increase the creation of banks of clouds as the cooler air over the sea is forced over the arc of Jabal Qara behind Al Balid which further drops the air temperature, in which clouds can grow.

Finally, a unique Seasonal Cloud Forest in the mountains catches the cloud's mist, which condenses over the leaves and branches, 'occult precipitation', and falls to the ground drop by drop. This precipitation of mist by the trees is likely a substantial proportion of the total addition to groundwater supplies to the coastal plain. Without the tree cover in the mountains, the water supply to the plain below will be substantially less.

The summer Monsoon results in a range of temperatures throughout the year in Salalah between 20-30c. This is much less variable than in other regions of Arabia.

In winter, the winds reverse as cooler air over northern India and Arabia flows out along Oman's coast from the northeast past Al Balid onto Somalia and the lands to its south. The predictable wind directions of summer and winter also powered sailing ships on return journeys across the seas.

CocoNut Plantations next to Al Balid

Al Balis is surrounded by an agricultural landscape of plantations of CocoNut Palms, with Banana and Papaya. Secondary crops such as beans, leaf vegetables and animal fodder create a year-round mosaic of greenery in a form of multi-level intensive farming.

*Oriental Garden Lizard*

These plantations are home to the Oriental Garden Lizard, *Calotes versicolor*, whose males have dramatic breeding colours during the pre-Monsoon period. Before the construction of the current stone edging to the *Khawr* at Al Balid the land east of the museum had areas of grass for fodder. The edge of the lagoon, especially the southern edge, now has Reed beds of *Phragmites australis* and Indian Almond tree *Terminalia catappa*. Salt marsh plants are widespread on the western arm of the lagoon; these include a type of Seablight, *Suaeda fruticose*, which, after drying and grinding, was used to add cheap volume to tobacco snuff. The dry, dusty central area has Desert Cotton, *Aerva javanica*, whose grey flower heads have been used to stuff pillows and to wrap and help heal flesh wounds. On the beach in front of Al Balid, expect to see a variety of birds, including Gulls, Heron, and Tern.

EXCAVATIONS WITHIN AL BALID HAVE FOUND BRONZE Age stone tools, including scrapers and blades. The site, whose remains we see today, appears to have gradually developed from AD 400. The development was possibly because of the decline of Samharam, or the anchorage at Raysut, to the west, where the modern Salalah Port has been built. This early development seems to have focused on the western area, with walling discovered around the *Husn* and '*Masjid Al Juma*' mosque from these early years.

After the Kingdom of Himyar, towards western Yemen, finally conquered the Hadhramaut in Yemen's east at the end of the 3rd century AD, Al Balid was at the eastern edge of the Yemeni Himyarite kingdom area of influence. This territory included much of the region where Frankincense still grows.

After the conquest of the Himyarite kingdom in AD527 by the Ethiopian kingdom of Aksum, Dhofar became independent. However, the Persian Sassanid commander Vahrez bin Kamjar landed in the Hadhramaut and conquered the Himyarite capital of Sana in AD570. The area around Al Balid likely was vassal to the Sassanian Empire. It was from this period that Al Balid grew as an important trading town.

From the period of the Prophet Mohammed (AD 571-632) the region was a part of the growing Islamic territory. However, as with many other areas in Arabia, Dhofar seceded from the rule of Mohammed's successor, the Caliph Abu Bakr. The general Ikrima bin Abu Jahl firmly brought the region back into the Islamic domain after the battles in Dhofar (known then as Mahra) in October 632 and Hadhramaut in January and February AD633 during the Ridda Wars.

Hidden away in the plantations opposite Al Balid's *Husn* is a tomb that is testimony to the stories associated with the flow of people through the region. It is known as the burial location of the legendary King of Kerala, Cheraman Perumal of Kodungalloor, now part of the southern Indian state of Kerala. The essence of the story attached to his tomb is that Cheraman Perumal had visited the Prophet Mohammed in Mecca, where he became a Muslim. During his return voyage to Kerala, King Perumal died and was buried in the tomb 600meters north of Al Balid.

Unfortunately, 'Cheraman Perumal' is a generic term for any monarch of the two Chola dynasties in Kerala. Neither dynasty appears to have ruled during the time of the Prophet Mohammed. The general story is part of the oral, malleable, history of Southern India, perhaps transported into Dhofar by people from Kerala. The tomb has a neighbour, that of 'Taj Al Din', the king's companion. The principal person buried has also been named as 'Abdul Rahman al Samiri' (died 831). Samiri is a generic term used locally for Hindus, so this person with his Muslim first name must have been a Hindu convert. The neighbour also has a variant of his name - 'Abu Bakr Taj Al Din'. Colonel S.B. Miles, the British representative to Oman, visited the tombs in 1884 and noted a version of the story. As of this publication's date, the tomb's mausoleum has been demolished.

The excavation at Al Balid has revealed Abbasid period ceramics, mainly from the western area. These have been dated from the period 750-900. Clearly, Al Balid had connections with the broader world in much the same way that Samharam had. Direct trade with China is illustrated by the Tang dynasty, 618–907, ceramics being excavated and from this period is the earliest Chinese mention of Al Balid as "Nu-fa". The volume of Chinese imports during this period was matched by exports of Frankincense resin to China, when in 1077, Guangzhou (Canton) alone imported 175 tons. From 950, Al Balid underwent further development with the *Masjid Al Juma* mosque, *Husn* and Town Wall being enlarged.

The rulers of Al Balid during this period were the 'Minjui' family, who, after having occupied Mirbat to the east of Salalah, moved to Al Balid. This dynasty is little studied but is thought to have come from the Iranian coast or possibly Balkh in northern Afghanistan.

The earliest known named ruler of Al Balid was Rashid bin Ahmed Al Minjui, who died in 1096. His son Abdulla bin Rashid succeeded as ruler. Al Balid appears to have been considered a military power as, in 1116, it received a delegation from the 'Kamar' tribe of southern Arabia asking for military help from the people of Al Balid. Around 1135, an expedition of 15 ships & 700 men arrived at Al Balid from the island of Kish off the Persian coast. At the time, Kish was the principal Iranian port for the Seljuks, in the area of modern Iran, Iraq and areas abutting them. However, the local vassal ruler of Kish was an Arab, Walad Al Amid, who was possibly from Yemen. He was intent on ransacking or capturing Aden, itself a vassal of the Fatimids in Egypt. Perhaps to get provisions, his force attacked Al Balid on the outward journey. Al Balid was thereafter regularly the focus of foreign interests.

For almost two months in 1200, an army from the Hadhramaut in Yemen unsuccessfully besieged the town before returning to the west. Soon after, the rule of the Minjui in Al Balid was broken by a native of the Hadhramaut, Ahmed bin Mahmood Al Himyari Al Haboodhi. He was a trader, and after being shipwrecked, he eventually became *Wazir*, Minister, for the Minjui ruler, whom he overthrew. Ahmed died in 1227, following which a succession of people ruled until, by 1258, another Minjui, Mohammed Abu Baqr Al Minjui, became the ruler of Al Balid. The town continued to be of interest to rulers from the north and Iran, for in 1261, Mahmood bin Ahmed Al Kashi Al Qalhati, the ruler of the island Kingdom of Hormuz at the entrance to the Arabian Gulf, fresh from occupying the town of Qalhat in northern Oman, pillaged Al Balid with his Turkish troops. Mohammed Abu Baqr Al Minjui eventually repulsed Al Qalhati. On the return north, Mahmood Al Qalhati tried to occupy the interior of northern Oman, using Qalhat as his base and lost 5,000 men, a sign of the army's size he used to attack Al Balid. Mohammed Abu Baqr rebuilt Al Balid with a re-fortified wall and four gates, renaming it Mansura, 'Victorious'.

Around 1271, another Al Haboodhi, Salim bin Idris Al Haboodhi, arrived from Hadhramaut and regained power for his family. After this, Salim also temporarily gained power in the Hadhramaut by sending relief food during famine. The ruler of the Hadhramaut gave Salim major forts there in exchange for the food. However, the people of Hadhramaut quickly recaptured these forts, which left Salim with a grudge that would become his downfall.

The downfall of Salim bin Idris involved Madhaffar bin Yousef (Al Muzaffar), the second Sultan (ruled 1249-1295) of the Yemeni Rasulid Dynasty who was based in Taiz in western Yemen, about 1200km from Al Balid. Shortly after Salim bin Idris lost the Hadhramaut, Sultan Madhaffar bin Yousef despatched an envoy to Persia by sea. Unfortunately, the ship was wrecked off the Dhofar coast. Salim seized the envoy's gifts in compensation for his loss in the Hadhramaut (a vassal state to Sultan Madhaffar bin Yousef), claiming God gifted these to him. Madhaffar bin Yousef then directed his Governor of Aden, the port south of Taiz, to send a naval attack in 1278 against Al Balid to enforce restitution of the envoy's baggage. The Governor of

Aden's flotilla was defeated in the attack and pursued back to Aden by Salim bin Idris.

Madhaffar bin Yousef then sent what must have been an overwhelming force, which moved on to Al Balid in three divisions, two by land and one by sea. On 14th December 1278, a battle was fought on the plain near the village of Awqad, about 12km west of Al Balid. Salim bin Idris, along with about 300 men, was slain, and 800 prisoners were taken. Following that victory, the town of Al Balid was occupied, the start of a long rule by the Rasulid Dynasty. Madhaffar appointed a son, Al Wathiq Nur Al Din Ibrahim, as ruler of Al Balid.

Al Wathiq was the ruler mentioned by Marco Polo in 1285 when he described Al Balid as "a great and noble and fine town with a Count for their chief, who is subject to the Soldan of Aden". Marco Polo continues to describe Al Balid; "It stands upon the sea and has a very good haven, so that there is a great traffic of shipping between this and India; and the merchants take hence great numbers of Arab horses to that market, making great profits thereby". The chronicler of the Rasulid dynasty, Ali Al Khazraji, describes Al Wathiq's town as having a mint, suggesting that it quickly gained some independence from his father. On Al Wathiq's death in 1311, a splendid pair of marble tombstones, sculpted in Khambhat Gujarat (India), were acquired to stand over his grave in Robat, two km inland from Al Balid. They are displayed within the National Museum, Muscat, on loan from the Victoria and Albert Museum London.

The Rasulids were considered vassals of the Mamluk rulers of Egypt & the Hijaz. Vast caravans of gifts were sent to Cairo, a tribute to the Mamluk Sultan from the Rasulids profitable trade, from as far away as China. Occasionally, the Sultans sent a return gift. In 1397, part of it included 30 Turkish Mamluks (soldiers), 12 fine Horses with their trappings, Anatolian and Armenian female slaves and an experienced Jewish physician from Egypt. Perhaps the 30 Mamluks were to train the Rasulid army.

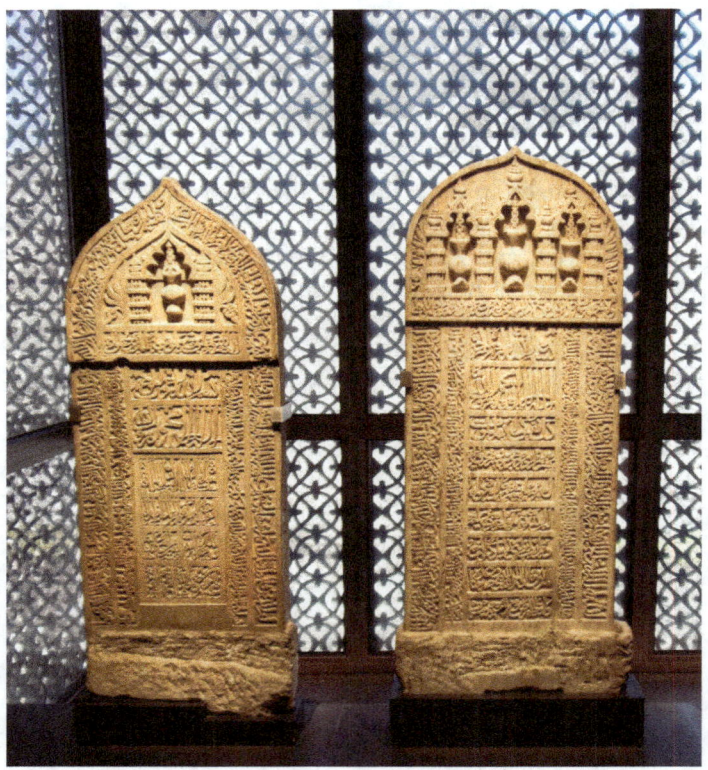

Gravestones - *Al Wathiq Nur Al Din Ibrahim - National Museum Muscat*

The predictable wind directions in the Indian Ocean allowed sailing ships to make lengthy voyages from one port to another throughout the Arabian Sea and the wider Indian Ocean area. Then, patiently waiting for the wind reversal, make the return voyage using these 'trade winds'. Notable arrivals after Marco Polo included Mohammed bin Abdullah Al Lawati, called Ibn Battuta, a Moroccan from Tangiers, who arrived in Al Balid two times by ship.

When Ibn Battuta visited Al Balid in c 1329, he found that the town's "The population of Al Balid are engaged in trading, and have no livelihood except from this. It is their custom that when a vessel arrives from India or elsewhere, the Sultan's slaves go down to the shore, and come out to the ship in a *Sambaq* [an Arabia Sea ship], carrying with them a complete set of robes for the owner of the vessel or his agent, and also for the '*Rubban*', who is the captain, and for the '*Kirazi*' who is the ship's writer.

Three horses are brought for them, on which they mount and ride, with drums and trumpets playing before them from the seashore to the Sultan's residence, where they make their salutations to the Wizier [Minister] and Amir Jandar [military chief]. Hospitality is supplied to all who are in the vessel for three nights, and when the three nights are up they eat in the Sultan's residence. These people do this in order to gain the goodwill of the ship-owners."

The merchants, who Ibn Battuta said, traded with Al Balid included people from "India, Yemen, and China" who purchased a range of products, including Frankincense resin, Horses and Honey made from Coconut sap" to take back to their lands. Ibn Battuta later visited China himself and revisited Al Balid in c 1346, again by sea, on his return journey from China, which eventually took him home to Morocco.

The merchants from distant China, commented about by Ibn Battuta, were followed by several visits to Al Balid between 1405-1433 by Chinese fleets under the Ming dynasty's admiral Zheng He. Describing the habits of the inhabitants of Al Balid, Zheng He's interpreters wrote, "every praying day (Friday) there is no trade in the market they burn gharu-wood, sandalwood and so on in the incense containers, people stand over it to fumigate their clothes and at last they go to pray. When people walk through the streets, the incense fragrances linger for a long time". Remarkably, the ruler was described as heading a procession that included not only Camels and Horses but also Elephants – an incredible parade given the compact size of Al Balid.

*An Arab ship by Yahya Al Wasiti (13th century) - the stitched hull can be seen*

The ruler of Al Balid sent envoys to accompany Zheng He on two of his return voyages to China despite the sea voyage being over 10,000 km. They travelled to Beijing and met the Yongle Emperor, Zhu Di (1402-1424) and his later successor, the Xuande Emperor, Zhu Zhanji (1425-1435). The Hongxi Emperor (1424-1425) discontinued the voyages. A range of gifts, including animals, some possibly from Oman, such as Leopard and Ostrich, and others from elsewhere, such as Giraffe and Rhinoceros, were carried as gifts from Al Balid and other lands.

The ruler of Al Balid in the early 15th century may have been Ali bin Omar bin Jaafar bin Badr Al Katheri from Hadhramaut, who occupied Dhofar from 1411.

Silting up of the lagoon in Al Balid caused larger ships to have difficulty berthing at the jetties from the start of the 14th century – despite evidence of dredging. The speed of silting up was probably accelerated by a drop in sea levels from 1400-1500. Natural problems were followed by the arrival of the Portuguese into the Arabian Sea. Their domination of the Arabian Sea, heralded the disruption of the centuries-old trade routes.

Portuguese fleets must have sailed past Al Balid frequently. In 1503, an expedition led by Vicente Sodre left the coast of southwest India, near Cochin. It arrived off Aden, capturing merchant ships. His ships then anchored off the Hallaniyyat Islands, east of Al Balid, where they sank in a storm. In 1507, Afonso de Albuquerque conquered the island of Socotra and coasted north along Oman's coast - up to Qurayyat and Muscat, which he conquered in July.

Remarkably, despite attempts in 1526 & 1553, the Portuguese never conquered Al Balid. This may have been because the Al Katheri rulers, of Hadhramaut, were allies of the Ottoman Turks. Sultan Badr bin Abdullah Al Katheri as a result had a partly Ottoman mercenary army. They used a form of matchlock, locally called Abu Fatila. A defence armed with gunpowder may have been just enough to ward off attacks.

After occupying Egypt in 1517 and finally capturing Aden in 1548, the Ottomans increased trade into their own ports. As trade was directed into ports governed by the Ottomans or Portuguese the viability of independent ports declined. In Al Balid, the ruler Badr bin Abdullah Al Katheri appears to have further reduced the town's trade during his rule of Al Balid from 1516 to 1569 by restricting the critical trade of Horses, Frankincense resin and Fish Oil. A significant storm, probably of cyclonic strength, at some time between 1600-1700 caused considerable damage in the southern areas of the town, and evidence of this is shown in sand deposits. The combined effect of a silted-up lagoon, trade disruption and storm damage must have made the inhabitants look for other locations to trade from.

Other foreign powers were also arriving in the region. In 1692 & 1705 and later, ships from England used Al Balid to get provisions. Unsurprisingly, given the Portuguese attacks and decimation of trade, they found the inhabitants less welcoming than those who received Ibn Battuta.

By late 1806, Sayyid Mohammed Akil ruled the town. He claimed descent from the Prophet Mohammed, adding to his prestige. Though born in Salalah, he was recently based in the

Red Sea on Kamaran island, Yemen, which he purchased, apparently on behalf of Napoleon's France - a forward base against British India. In April 1806, after successful naval action against the merchant ship 'Essex' from Salem USA, off Kamaran, and the slaughter of all its men, he withdrew to Muscat. After disputes in Muscat, Sayyid Mohammed Akil settled in Mirbat, Dhofar, where he built the castle. By 1824, his influence extended west along the coast for around 400km from Al Balid. However, in March 1829, a group of armed men attacked and killed him near Mirbat.

Following the death of Sayyid Mohammed Akil, the ruler of northern Oman, Sultan Said bin Sultan Al Said was invited to assume rule in Dhofar. He sent a force ahead of his own arrival. He then withdrew completely to quell a rebellion in his East African port of Mombasa. The Dhofar region disintegrated into tribal areas ruled by the Sheikh of that area.

As Britain's navy started the switch from sail to steam power, increased coastal surveys of Dhofar took place. In 1834, Palinurus, a survey ship, anchored off Raysut. The British naval captain Stafford Haines led a group from the boat and described the route from 'Haffer' (Al Haffa) to Robat (northeast of Al Balid) without mentioning Al Balid. The town had decayed into unimportance.

In 1846, the Palinurus again anchored off the coast so that her crew could further increase Britain's information regarding the area. Assistant surgeon H.J. Carter accompanied a team as they traversed the coastal plain. He was more observant than Haines and found that; "On the south eastern coast of Arabia, in the district of Dofar, are the ruins of El Balad, situated on the shore, in Lat. 17' 1' N and Long. 54' 12' 30" E., between the towns of Silalah, and El Hafa on the west, and that of Dareez on the east, separated from the latter by a grassy plain of more than a mile in extent, and from the former by the same distance of richly cultivated ground. In front, a narrow slip of sandy beach divides them from the sea. Behind them, the level plain of Dofar stretches back to a lofty range of mountains, forming this district's inland boundary. The ruins, sited within one hundred yards of the sea, are spread over an area of two miles long, and six hundred yards broad, and comprise extensive mounds of loose hewn stones, worn and blackened by long exposure to the weather. Groups of columns surmount each mound, with capitals, shafts, pedestals, and fragments of ornamental sculpture, strewed around them; and occasionally troughs, used for baths; all of which having been skilfully worked out of solid blocks of freestone, give an air of costliness and importance to the remains of this city, which, contrasted with the dilapidated state that the whole now assumes, forcibly recalls to the imagination the activity, wealth, and prosperity, which but a few centuries ago existed where now there is nothing but a vast accumulation of desolate, dismal, and unfrequented ruins."

During another period of increased instability in Dhofar in 1879, the leading tribal Sheikhs in Dhofar invited Oman's Sultan, Turki Al Said, to rule the region. His forces stayed and its from this invitation that Dhofar became part of modern Oman.

Wendell Phillips made limited in-scope excavations in the west of Al Balid in the 1950s. As was the case with his archaeological excavations at Samharam, no academic publication was made. Subsequent excavations at Al Balid have been undertaken with the supervision of the Government of Oman. The University of Naples, led by Dr Paolo Costa, dug at two areas, including the principal *Masjid Al Juma* mosque, in 1978-1981. In 1997, the University of Aachen, led by Prof Michael Jansen, documented, and partially excavated many buildings in the west of the town until 2003. From 2005-2012, Dr Juris Zarins & Dr Lynn Newton excavated the southern wall along with a couple of previously unexamined buildings. The University of Naples has been excavating at Al Balid since 2021.

The renewed recent interest in Al Balid with the extensive archaeological examination culminated in the town being included in the inscription by UNESCO of the Land of Frankincense World Heritage Site on the 2nd December 2000.

∽

## AL BALID'S PHYSICAL SITES

**THE MODERN ENTRANCE TO AL BALID.**

Extending along the coast for 1500 metres, Al Balid is set on what was, essentially, a small coastal U-shaped lagoon. The water acted as a moat and gave a shallow harbour to the town's north, east and west. The sea was to the south, together they provided the town with one of the more defensible sites on the coastal plain. Most archaeological remains are from the town's prime trading period from the 10th to 16th centuries AD.

A principal entrance into the historic ancient town was by the bridge in the west section of the lagoon, close to the *Husn* and main mosque. Today, modern bridges allow visitors to cross the lagoon into the northern section of the town.

**SITE-A The Museum of the Frankincense Land**, within Al Balid, focuses on the history of Oman in one hall, emphasising the crucial role of Frankincense resin. In contrast, the second hall covers the maritime history and the traditional boats of Oman.

Gift Shops

To the rear and outside the main museum's buildings are modern shops, relocated in 2022 from within the museum. This location, from a retailer's perspective, could be better. Opening hours may be shorter than the main site.

**HISTORY HALL**

Ahead, beyond the Frankincense tree in the central courtyard, the **History Hall** immediately engages a visitor with a topographic 3D representation featuring Oman's UNESCO World Heritage Sites and other places of interest in Oman. In the adjacent area, an overview of Oman's remarkable history is given with stone tools, dated between 1,000,000-700,000 years ago from Wadi Ghadun, and more finely worked flint from the same *wadi* but dated to 3500-2500 BC illustrating the extraordinary timespan of Oman's human history.

*Museum of the Frankincense Land*

More recent periods of history include the culture associated with the proto-historic settlement at Bat, northern Oman. Before the time of the pyramids of Egypt, Copper was mined in northern Oman's mountains and exported to the ancient cities of Mesopotamia, a journey by land and sea of some two thousand kilometres. It was exported in small nuggets shaped like bread buns, examples of which are shown from Bahla and dated to 2500-2000 BC. A small black piece of Bitumen from Ras Al Jinz again draws attention to those ancient links with Mesopotamia, the region's primary source of Bitumen, just as modern Iraq is still a major oil producer. Impressed on the surface of the Bitumen is a pattern formed by bundles and mats of woven reeds, the outer surface of ancient Boats, which were then caulked with a Bitumen mix to waterproof them. A delicate Ivory Hair Comb and various well-worked jewellery pieces from the trading settlement at Ras Al Jinz in northeastern Oman illustrate ancient communication between Oman and the Indus Valley civilisation.

The bronze Snakes from Salut, the Bronze and Iron Age fortification in northern Oman, are displayed in the museum. These snakes are comparable in style to the carved snake motifs on a stone shrine discovered in Samharam. As these representations of Snakes are realistic enough, they almost certainly are *Echis omanensis* vipers.

Chinese pottery shards discovered at Al Balid show the trade with China. These are mostly dated between the 12th and 15th centuries and include green celadon and later blue and white Chinese ceramics. The chess pieces found at Ash Shisr have been included here, they are a (in English terms used today) pawn, a king, a bishop, a knight, and a castle. More ancient are the flint tools from Ash Shisr, including spear points, axes, and arrowheads, from 7000-6000 BC.

Central to the museum is the area focusing on the Frankincense resin trade. An easy-to-understand display shows the retail varieties of the resin itself, and alongside are archaeological finds, which not only suggest the important religious and cultural role of burning Frankincense resin but also illustrate the wildlife which may have inhabited the region. Lions feature on bronze and stone burners alongside Ibex, which until recently were the focus of ritualised hunting in southern Arabia. After the area Frankincense room the central role of Islam in Oman is explained in the area a. The letter said to have been sent from the Prophet Mohammed, inviting the joint rulers of Oman and the Omani people to convert to Islam, is shown in a facsimile. Finely executed Qurans from the 10th to 19th centuries , the historical book 'Kashf Al Ghummah' (published as Annuls of Oman in English), and medical books are among the religious and cultural highlights.

A fitting final section illustrates Oman's modern development during the reign of Sultan Qaboos, especially its human development, focusing on education and Oman's developing legal framework.

**OMAN AS A MARITIME NATION.**

Next to the History Hall is the **Maritime Hall**, which focuses on Oman's maritime history. A hypothetical reconstruction of a mid-third millennium BC boat used in the Arabian Gulf is among the beautifully made scale models.

*Examples of Arabian Sea Ship's hulls*

The third millennium was when Bitumen was used to waterproof boats. Unlike European boats, which are named for their sails, Omani boats are differentiated by their hulls. However, today, the generic term Dhow is used for Arab boats by non-Arabs. The museum covers all types of Omani craft. This includes the *Shasha*, a small boat less than 2 meters long, made from date palm leaf, used for fishing close to the shore in northern Oman, to the wooden *Baghla*, up to 40 metres in length and 400 tons in weight.

One of the features of Omani boats, until relatively recently, was that they were constructed not with nails but using a technique of sewing the planks together with natural plant fibres. This method was employed in ancient boats, such as the Khufu ship unearthed in the Giza necropolis, Egypt, and dated around 2,500 BC. Sewn ships were used into the 20$^{th}$ century by Omani sailors. In 2010, a full-scale 18meter long sewn boat, Jewel of Muscat, sailed from Muscat to Singapore as a gift from the Government of Oman to the people of Singapore. She was built from evidence of the 'Belitung Wreck', an early medieval Arab boat wrecked around AD830 off Indonesia. It carried a full cargo of luxury ceramics and metalware from China. It would be nice if it were destined for Al Balid, but the logical destination would have been the capital of the Islamic Empire, Baghdad, or at a stretch to the regional Egyptian capital of the period, Al Askar (now within modern Cairo).

Also on display at the Maritime Hall are stone ships anchors. These have been recovered from the sea near Al Balid and elsewhere in Oman's coastal regions, notably Qalhat in the north. They weigh up to one ton and have three holes: one to allow a rope to attach the anchor to the ship and two for wooden flukes to grab onto the seabed.

*Ship's Stone Anchor*

**SITE-B** Immediately west of the Museum of the Frankincense Land is a 'Scientific Model of Wadi Dawkah', the UNESCO site with Frankincense Trees, beyond the mountains to the north of Salalah. Trees here, at Al Balid, are also Frankincense. They were planted in 2008 and irrigated with drip feed irrigation, allowing for relatively rapid growth. This is a most convenient location to get close to Frankincense Trees. The central stone feature is a Bronze Age monument.

**SITE-C** West of the modern east bridge (the closest bridge to the museum) is a bastion and gate within the northern wall beside the lagoon. The gate may mark a boundary between Al Balid's built up area to the west and less heavily developed east and the eastern end of the original town wall.

**site-D** Walking west after crossing the east bridge, along the path parallel to the lagoon, a building on the left with seven or eight rooms on the ground floor surrounding a small courtyard has been excavated. Its layout is a typical merchants' house built in trading towns such as Salalah or Mokha on Yemen's Red Sea coast until the mid-20th century. On the ground floor, these buildings would have comprised a reception area for visiting merchants. Here would be adjacent storage areas and animal shelters, and the upper floors would have private accommodation for the family or staff.

**Site-E** This is one of the numerous mosques within Al Balid. With 16 columns and a Minaret it must have been built by a wealthy individual or family. The Mihrab adds to the impression of wealth, as it was built from wood, presumably imported, as fine quality wood is scarce in the region. Six graves are within the enclosure of the mosque, this proximity suggests that these are the family connected with the mosque. To the east of the entrance is a water well and basins to allow ritual ablution before prayer. This complex dates to the 13th century.

**site-F** A small, walled cemetery lies east of Al Balid's principal mosque. There are some 300 graves within this tightly packed cemetery, and they have a range of headstone styles, some inscribed with names and others with cultural symbols. Two larger historical cemeteries lie outside the town walls; one is immediately west of the bridge over the moat near *Husn* Al Balid, and the other at Robat, two km northeast of the town (this is in a private area), is where the gravestone for Wathiq Nur Al Din Ibrahim, now in the National Museum – Muscat, was located.

**site-G** East of the *Husn* is a small mosque that had eight columns. Probably founded around 850 with two further construction periods, this is one of 36 mosques that originally lay within the town walls. To the east of this mosque is a water well for ablutions, and to the northwest is the location of its Minaret. As with most of these mosques, there is evidence of food consumption within the building. The practice of holding major celebratory within a mosque is still common in many settlements within Oman, and this evidence in Al Balid suggests that it is an old historical practice. As with *Husn* Al Balid, this mosque was built above one of many Iron Age buildings scattered in Al Balid's western area.

Gravestone - Al Balid

**SITE-H** The principal mosque of Al Balid is a '*Masjid Al Juma*' used for Friday midday prayers and other prayers. As is customary for mosques throughout Oman, the mosque sits on a terrace; here, it's about one meter high.

Possibly built in the 9th century and certainly in use by the 11th century , the mosque remained in use until the 17th century. Al Balid's *Masjid Al Juma* seems to have been refurbished several times, including the alteration, and reinforcing of the main *Qibla* wall and adding a Minaret on the north of that wall.

Masjid Al Juma from Al Husn

Over 140 pillars were used within the building, creating a hypostyle mosque. Representations of the original columns have been placed where they stood. Those columns in this *Masjid Al Juma* had a fleur-de-lis decoration at their capital. This design appears on many of the columns scattered throughout Al Balid. A small open-roofed courtyard, which in Oman is called a '*shamsiya*', was set in the centre of the building to allow light and air into the mosque's interior.

Throughout the building, walls were plastered with a thick coating of *Sarooj* (lime-based stucco), which added structural support and permitted finer decoration than coarse-grained stone allows. Above the stone columns, arched wooden timbers supported the flat roof. Bertram Thomas took photographs in 1929 of this mosque, which appear to show the remains of arches on some columns. This *Masjid Al Juma* has two Minarets, one to its northeast and one at the northwest. In the southeast of the mosque is a small room with a *Mihrab* (the semi-circular niche that indicates the *Qibla* direction), a possible prayer area for women.

Masjid Al Juma

Ibn Battuta described the ruler of Al Balid going to the mosque from the *Husn* for Friday mid-day prayers "The Sultan himself does not go out, nor is he seen by anyone except on

Fridays, when he goes out for the midday prayer, and then returns to his residence, but he prevents no one from entering the audience-hall. The Amir Jandar [military chief] sits at its door, and it is to him that every person with a petition or a grievance presents his case; he sends it for the Sultan's consideration, and the reply comes to him at once." The *Mihrab* wall, to the west, has what may have been an exclusive entrance for the town's ruler and his entourage, either side of the *Mimbar* (pulpit) set in the northwest *Qibla* wall (direction for prayer towards the *Kaaba* in Mecca). Entering here was more convenient if arriving from the *Husn*; it also meant the ruler could pray in the front row of the congregation, immediately in front of the *Mihrab*. This access, through the *Qibla* wall, is used, for example, in the Sultan Qaboos Grand Mosque in Muscat, where the Royal entrance is from within the Mihrab.

In Al Bilad, the other entrances to this mosque are on the east, north, and south walls were for the general population and were indeed preferred for religious reasons. The northern wall had six doors, and the southern wall had seven doors, which not only allowed access but also must have allowed a continual flow of air through the prayer room.

Today, entrance to this *Masjid Al Juma* is still made via one of three flights of stairs, each leading to a doorway set into the *Qibla* wall.

To the south of the *Masjid Al Juma* a rapid growth of the vegetation has taken place. This results from the 2018 Cyclone Mekunu, whose rainfall in Salalah was over 61 cm.

GeoTextile - Al Husn Al Balid

**SITE-I** The *Husn* (*Husn* is the word used in Oman for castle) of Al Balid is opposite a second modern bridge in the western part of the town. Rising to four or more floors in height the *Husn* comprised an array of rooms built around an open courtyard. It was probably constructed in the mid-10th century over an earlier Iron Age structure. Now, as in historic times, the main entrance into the *Husn* is close to its southwest tower. The access stairs ascended from the town's main square through substantial gates. With the stair's broad and shallow slope, pack animals could enter into warehousing on a lower floor, or the ruler's choice of rising animal could ascend to the upper floors. The requirement to allow access for a favourite animal, typically a horse, was a common design feature in castles in Oman until the 20th century.

Deposits of ash mixed with bronze found within the *Husn* suggest that weapons were manufactured and repaired within the building. The *Husn's* defences included towers on three corners and a barrier wall on the remaining corner, which extended from the *Husn* towards the main northern town wall. This extension also had rooms.

Excavations on the upper part of the *Husn* show rooms that appear domestic in size and layout, rather than a size to hold a large gathering of people. The towers were added as a defence in the late 15th century, after the widespread introduction of canon (an example of a small hand-held canon found here can be seen in the Museum). On the northeast corner, buttressing supported what must have been a collapsing outer wall, a precursor to the overall decay of the *Husn*. An impression of its possible appearance comes from the smaller Al Katheri Palace in Seiyun Hadhramaut. Although completed in the early 20$^{th}$ century, this probably dates, in origin, to the reign of Badr bin Abdullah Al Katheri (known as Badr Abu Tuwayriq), who also ruled Al Balid.

North of *Husn* Al Balid is an area that is assumed to have been the housing and accommodation for people working in the *Husn*. This proximity allowed them to quickly get immediate protection if there was an attack; it also separated the housing from the commercial areas on the southern sides of Al Balid.

Upper layer - Al Husn Al Balid

**SITE-J** *Al Furda* & **SITE-K** Al Balid Western Gate are south of *Husn* Al Balid. Immediately west of the *Masjid Al Juma* was *Al Furda* (Customs House) and the adjacent original Western Gate and Town Bridge. The function of *Al Furda* was the physical assessment of the value of imported goods and then the imposition of customs duty or calculation of a share of the profit, which provided income to the ruler. Most of these goods were high-value products, including Gold and Rhinoceros Horns. The town's main suq appears to have been west of the lagoon, outside the town's wall. Close to the town's gate was a quay allowing boats to be unloaded into the assessment area; Chinese coins and carbon dating suggest this was built around the mid-9th century. This lagoon area appears to have silted up by the early 15th century.

**SITE-L** The town's Bridge, which leads into the western area of Al Balid, spanned part of the lagoon, and gave easy access to the west of the town, including the *Al Furda*. The lagoon here was originally around 15 meters wide, and the size of the columns suggests the volume of people and goods transported across. The columns varied shapes suggest that they were taken from abandoned buildings in Al Balid. The bridge dates from 950-1200 and sits over an older complex associated with a gateway.

Column with Fleur de Lys decoration

**SITE-M** In the southwestern corner of Al Balid is a double platform that is assumed to be either a lighthouse or lookout tower; perhaps it served as both.

**SITE-N** Close to the Lighthouse is the Southwestern Gate Complex. This dates to, at the earliest, 750. The well-dressed stone is comparable to the blocks on other sea facing gates. Just to the north of the Southwestern Gate Complex are the remains of a large building, which may be of around the same date as this Complex; at a later date, a mosque was built over this large building. The general area of the complex overlays a development dated to the Iron Age.

**SITE-O** On the southern wall, close to its western end, is a Circular Bastion. The lagoon's exit may previously have been broad enough that this bastion marked its eastern edge at the exit into the sea near the Southwestern Gate Complex. Drains built into the wall reduce the impact of waves by allowing some water to move through. Around 1300, a building was constructed over this bastion, perhaps after the lagoon had reduced in width and the military effectiveness had been eliminated.

*Southwestern Gate Complex - Al Balid*

**SITE-P** Sitting outside the southern town wall, towards its western edge, is a complex of buildings. This Complex was built at a period when a lagoon immediately south of the wall had silted up. To the east of this Complex is a large building with a central double staircase that gives private access from the north, directly from the town, and south of the building towards the sea gates. Finds in the building include simple carved human faces, which, along with water basins and drainage, suggest a communal building, possibly associated with rituals. About 20 meters west of this large Complex is a square mosque that would have allowed prayers without entering Al Balid.

**SITE-Q** The southern town wall stretches west to east for some 1,200 meters and is now set back from the sea, although the sea may have been closer during the town's trading period. During extreme tides, especially during the Monsoon season the sea must have pounded against the walls. Eventually, with 4 breakwaters, 17 towers and 3 town gates, it would have quelled both waves and attackers and impressed visitors.

**SITE-R** There are three gateways on the southern wall. Between the exterior Complex of buildings and the central jetty is a substantial entrance; its steps rise up the southern wall, which is made from monolithic blocks. Just after the central jetty, the second gate used a zigzag entrance that is so common in southern Arabian fortifications. The final gate was a postern gate just before the eastern jetty.

**SITE-S** In the central area of the southern wall is probably its most prominent feature, a substantial breakwater. This was a later attachment to a tower that was part of the original town wall. It may have been required due to changes in the access to the town from a seaside lagoon, requiring substantial new building works.

Al Balid Southern Wall

**SITE-T** A breakwater cum jetty dominates the eastern part of the southern wall. Projecting 38m beyond the southern wall, the breakwater extends to other walls, including the eastern seawall, the complex southeast of Al Balid and an elevated 'walkway' stretching north.

Bored holes into the breakwater break up water impact against the stone. The breakwater had a wooden jetty that added several meters length to its southern tip. The jetty's posts were supported on the many stone slabs that now cover the ground to the south of the stone breakwater. Each slab weighs around half a ton, and the holes bored into each slab hold the upright supports for the jetty and allowed for the stone's initial positioning. Carbon dating of wooden remains suggests a date of 750-950 for the jetty's construction. The size of the breakwater and the jetty structure shows that Ocean capable ships berthed directly here. It may also have allowed ships to be tied up and repaired at low tide, along the lines of a dry dock. By the time of Ibn Battuta, the silting of the lagoon and beach changes meant larger boats were anchored offshore, and smaller boats ferried goods to the jetty.

Breakwater and Jetty area

**SITE-U** The eastern extension of the southern wall included a large walled enclosure. This walled enclosure was accessed to its east by a gate, the principal entry into Al Balid's southeast Complex. The three rooms here may represent an administration area. It is possible that goods could be directly loaded through this gate into ships, as it has been speculated that this was the export area for goods, such as Frankincense resin and re-exports from Al Balid.

**SITE-V** To the north of the walled enclosure complex is an extension to it. The purpose of this area is open to speculation; it includes a dam structure, with sluice gates, on its western wall that captured naturally flowing spring water in the same area.

**SITE-W** Just to the west of the car park is a small collection of original wooden boats. If you have the time, the stitching used to secure the planks is worth looking at. This is a remnant of the time when Arabian Sea boat's timbers were stitched together, with no metal nails used.

**SITE-X** Accessed to the southeast (rear) of the Museum of the Frankincense Land, on the edge of the lagoon, is a covered shelter that is an excellent viewing point to watch the birds on the growth on the opposite side of the lagoon. You can reasonably expect to see Cattle Egret, *Bubulcus ibis* (perched on the Indian Almond tree) Western Reef Heron, *Egretta gularis*, Coot, *Fulica atra*, Little Grebe, *Tachybaptus ruficollis*, & Moorhen, *Gallinula chloropus*.

Stitching on Boat - Al Balid

**SITE-Y** is accessed by walking from the northeast (rear) of the Museum of the Frankincense Land, and north around the lagoon is a rather regimented Botanic Garden with native and near native plants of Dhofar. This is off the normal visitor area and poorly signed, but it is useful if you have ample time to spare, and will explore Dhofar.

**SITE-Z** Beyond the Botanic Garden is an elevated viewing platform on the lagoon's edge. Although it gives good views over to the Anantara Hotel, the result of the walk to it is not especially rewarding.

Not included in this A-Z is the elevated walkway parallel with the southern wall. Attached to the walkway are 8 buildings for cafes; a couple have functioning establishments. This substantial modern construction, unfortunately, acts as a barrier between Al Balid and its ancient highway, the Arabian Sea.

Cattle Egret - Indian Almond Tree - Al Balid

Viewing platform - Al Balid

## Visiting Al Balid 17.009409, 54.135681

If there is only one location you have time to visit in Salalah, Al Balid should be it.

Today, the remains of a castle, mosques and town wall can be explored in Al Balid, along with the Museum of the Frankincense Land, which explains the area's history and maritime heritage. Add in ease of access to the site, the Frankincense trees growing in Al Balid, Birdwatching and Gift Shops and you have a rounded experience.

The sites included at Al Balid above are arranged as an anticlockwise walk in the order you will meet them on that walk. Excluding the final three sites, the walk is more than four km; a bottle of water should be taken, and the heat and humidity will be a factor, as you will be walking in direct sun for over an hour. Although walking off the paths is tempting, the soil is dry, dusty silt and will get inside any footwear. If walking is not possible, there is a Golf Cart type chauffeured service, where you get a chance to see some places, there is also a Boating option.

Al Balid is on the coast in central Salalah on Sultan Qaboos St. Entry is by ticket purchased from the kiosk, after parking your car in the car park, or walking through and paying - as a non-resident of Oman OMR3 (child OMR1).

# MORE READING

**More reading**
- A Port in Arabia Between Rome and the Indian Ocean / Alessandra Avanzini / 8882654699
- Arabia Felix: Across the Empty Quarter of Arabia / Bertram Thomas / 978-1838075637
- Arabian Sands / Sir Wilfred Thesiger / 141442077
- Atlantis of the Sands / Sir Ranulph Fiennes / 747513279
- Oman / Tony Walsh / 978-1784776800
- Plants of Dhofar, the Southern Region of Oman / A. G. Miller / 715708082
- Southern Arabia / Theodore Bent / Smith, Elder & Co
- The Land of Incense / Juris Zarins / Sultan Qaboos University Publications
- The Road to Ubar: Finding the Atlantis of the Sands. / Nicholas Clapp / 285634763
- The Travels of Ibn Battuta / Rev Samuel Lee / 0486437655
- Unknown Oman / Wendel Phillips / Librairie Du Liban

Images by Tony Walsh - except
Augustus as a Pharaoh offering incense - Temple of Kalabsha Egypt - Lassi, Ebers Papyrus - Einsamer Schütze , Queen Hatshepsut Punt Expedition - Unknown, Three Magi - Chester M. Wood

*Frankincense Granules for Sale*

# ARABIC LANGUAGE

**ARABIC**

Transliteration of Arabic into English is an imperfect process. Arabic includes letters for sounds that have no corresponding one in English. Printed media, such as general books or newspapers, rarely use diacritics to show short vowels, but books where pronunciation is essential, such as the Quran, include them. Diacritics in writing were introduced in AD 791, by the Omani Al Khalil Al Farahidi, after the Quran was delivered in its spoken form and initially written without them. It's the written version of the Quran, with all its diacritics, that acts as an anchor to Arabic today.

There is also a wide variety of Arabic dialects, which have different pronunciations of the same word, in much the same way as, for example, British English and American English pronounce 'Tomato' differently. A simple but straightforward example is the Arabic for Mountain جبل. Jbel or Djebel are possible Latin alphabet transliterations for names in Morocco, like Djebel Sahrho. In Egypt and Sudan, the word is usually Gebel, as in Gebel Barkal. In the Arabian Gulf, the word for it is Jabal or Jebel, like Jabal Qara. The Arabic letters (and unwritten but known diacritics) remain the same; the regional pronunciation results in a different transliteration.

Historically, Arabic letters used in non-Arab languages, such as Persian, Ottoman Turkish, or Urdu, have also complicated the matter. Victorian academics may have learnt Arabic through teachers in those regions. Each of these historical language pronunciations has its own pronunciation characteristic, where, for instance, the Arabic word وزير, correctly used as "Minister" in those regions, was written as "Vizier" in English books like 1001 Nights. Today's modern transliteration from Arabic is Wazir.

A similar variety occurs in place names used in this book. When writing the Bradt Guide 4th & 5th Editions, I use the official Oman Government cartographic English spelling versions. The guidebook and Oman maps having the same place name spellings should make locations easier to check for visitors. I have also chosen to use the same approved spellings within this book. An example is Khawr Rawri, the approved Oman Government spelling, often Latinized as Khor Rori, including within the UNESCO list. Below are variants of words and place names listed in a glossary.

| Name in Book | Arabic | Translation | Alternative Names |
|---|---|---|---|
| Ain | عين | Ayn | Water Spring, in geography |
| Ayn Hamran | عين حمران | | Ain Hamran |
| Al Balid | البليد | | Al Baleed |
| Andhur | أنظور | | |
| Ash Shuwaymiyyah | الشويمية | | Shuwaymiyyah |
| Dhofar | ظفار | | Zufar |

Dhofar is Oman's largest region by area at 99,300sq km. Its population was 455,000 in October 2018 - a population density of 4.58 people per square km; most are in the coastal and sea-facing mountain regions.

| Name in Book | Arabic | Translation | Alternative Names |
|---|---|---|---|
| Dhofar Mountains | جبال ظفار | | Jabal Dhofar |
| Hanun | حنون | | Hanoon |
| Hormuz | هرمز | | Hurmuz |
| Jabal | جبل | Mountain | |
| Jabal Qara | جبل القرا | | |
| Khareef | الخريف | Autumn | |

In Dhofar, the Khareef is officially expected from 21st June to 21st September - the Monsoon season.

| Name in Book | Arabic | Translation | Alternative Names |
|---|---|---|---|
| Khawr | خور | Lagoon, Creek | Khor |
| Khawr Rawri | خور روري | | Khor Rori |
| Mirbat | مرباط | | |
| Monsoon | ريح موسمية | | |
| Mughsayl | المغسيل | | Al Mughsayl / Mughsail |

| Name in Book | Arabic | Translation | Alternative Names |
|---|---|---|---|
| Qalhat | قلهات | | Kalhat |
| Salalah | صلالة | | |

Salalah - This is Dhofar's largest town by far, with a population of 375,000. The city provides primary services for the region, including Airport, Seaport - along with Hospitals, Police and major hotels.

| Name in Book | Arabic | Translation | Alternative Names |
|---|---|---|---|
| Ash Shisr | الشصر | | Shisr /Shasr |
| Samharam | سمهرم | | Sumhuram / Sumhurum |
| Taqah | طاقة | | Taqa |
| Thumrayt | ثمريت | | Thumrait |

Thumrayt - The principal town on the desert side of the Dhofar Mountain range. There is a small Hospital, Police Station and other services, including simple hotels and restaurants.

| Name in Book | Arabic | Translation | Alternative Names |
|---|---|---|---|
| Til / Tilal | تل/تلال | Hill / Hills | |
| Ubar | أوبار | | Wabar, Awbar; also an associated name, Iram |
| *Wadi* | وادي | Valley | Wady |

*Wadi* - A deep canyon or a barely perceptible depression; the critical requirement is that it is a geographical area where water can flow through. The Nile Valley is Wadi Al Neel.

| Name in Book | Arabic | Translation | Alternative Names |
|---|---|---|---|
| Wadi Dawkah | وادي دوكة | | Wadi Dawqah |
| **Name in Book** | **Arabic** | **Translation** | **Alternative Names** |

If you leave a review of your thoughts about this book, other people will know if the book is right for them.

## Thank you 🙏

I do hope you enjoyed exploring The Land of Frankincense with this guide.

Tony

Copyright 2018

© All Rights Reserved. No part of this book may be reproduced or utilized in any form or by any means, electronic or mechanical, including photocopying, recording, or by any information storage and retrieval system, without permission in writing from the publisher and author.

Care has been taken to provide accurate information in this publication. Responsibility for making use of the information and any consequential loss, injury, mortality, or inconvenience is that of the reader or user. The author or publisher does not assume it.

Arabesque

www.ingramcontent.com/pod-product-compliance
Lightning Source LLC
Chambersburg PA
CBHW070100080526
44586CB00013B/1135